LAUGHING
at the
DEVIL

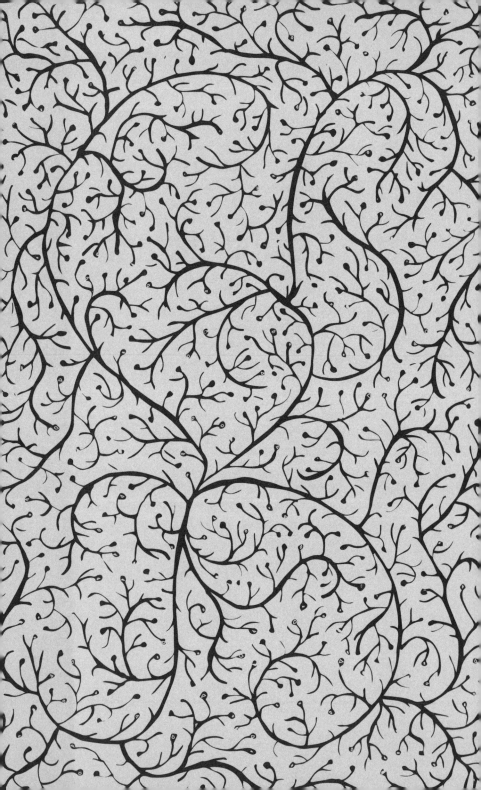

LAUGHING
at the
DEVIL

SEEING THE
WORLD WITH
Julian of Norwich

AMY LAURA HALL

DUKE UNIVERSITY PRESS

DURHAM AND LONDON   2018

© 2018 Duke University Press
All rights reserved
Printed in the United States of America on acid-free paper ∞
Designed by Heather Hensley
Typeset in Quadraat Pro by Copperline Book Services

Library of Congress Cataloging-in-Publication Data
Names: Hall, Amy Laura, author.
Title: Laughing at the devil : seeing the world with Julian of Norwich /
Amy Laura Hall.
Description: Durham : Duke University Press, 2018. |
Includes bibliographical references and index.
Identifiers: LCCN 2017049757 (print)
LCCN 2017060635 (ebook)
ISBN 9781478002109 (ebook)
ISBN 9781478000129 (hardcover : alk. paper)
ISBN 9781478000259 (pbk. : alk. paper)
Subjects: LCSH: Julian, of Norwich, 1343– | Great Britain—
History—Medieval period, 1066–1485. | Mysticism—History—
Middle Ages, 600–1500.
Classification: LCC BV4832.3 (ebook) | LCC BV4832.3 .H355 2018
(print) | DDC 282.092—dc23
LC record available at https://lccn.loc.gov/2017049757

Cover art and book illustrations by Julienne Alexander

For my parents,
Robert and Carol Hall

Just because I am a woman,

must I therefore believe that

I must not tell you about the

goodness of God, when I saw

at the same time both his

goodness and his wish that

it should be known?

—JULIAN OF NORWICH,
Revelations of Divine Love

CONTENTS

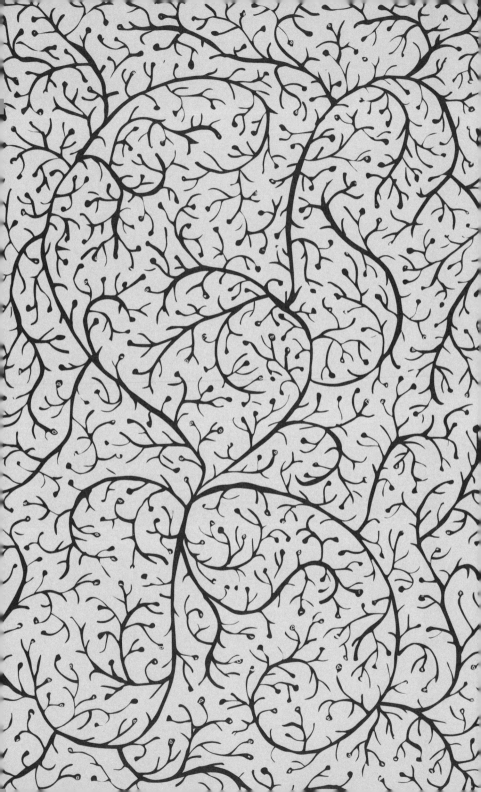

PREFACE
Devil: Zero

I also saw our Lord scorn [the Devil's] wickedness and set
him at nought, and he wants us to do the same. At this revelation I laughed heartily and that made those who were
around me laugh too, and their laughter pleased me. I wished
that my fellow Christians had seen what I saw, and then
they would all have laughed with me. But I did not see Christ
laughing. Nevertheless, it pleases him that we should laugh
to cheer ourselves, and rejoice in God because the Fiend has
been conquered.

—JULIAN OF NORWICH, *Revelations of Divine Love*

Rejoice?
But I did not see Christ laughing.
The Fiend has been conquered?
The Lord has made the Devil into nought, into a no-thing?
What does it mean to laugh at the Devil? To believe that "the Fiend has
been conquered"?
What does it mean to live not governed by fear?

Julian of Norwich is the medieval anchorite who taught me the
courage to look evil in the eye. Here are the fundamentals a new
reader needs to know about her: Julian of Norwich wrote two books

that, when bound together, fit in a coat pocket. As far as we can ascertain, Julian is the first woman to write a book in English. She was born in 1342. She received a series of visions from God in 1373, while she was on what she and others around her thought would be her deathbed. It took Julian two decades to sort out what she first saw when God granted her visions of love and truth. This is the reason we have a Short Text (ST) and a Long Text (LT) describing what she saw.[1] She wrote down her visions soon after she received them (the Short Text), and then took her time to think about how to write what is referred to as the Long Text. It took her years and years to think about the ramifications of what she had seen. We know Julian became an anchorite at St. Julian's Church in Norwich by 1393. This means that, by the time she was around fifty years old, she had dedicated herself to living the rest of her life in rooms attached to this busy church, centrally located in a port city. Her rooms faced a busy road. The fact that Julian eventually committed to live in a local church strikes some contemporary readers as remarkable. I am fascinated most by her extraordinarily unconfined visions, as she testified to a God uncontrolled by the strictures of her time and my own. Also Julian of Norwich laughed at the Devil.

I have come to hear Julian's laughter as a call to holy audacity. She received her delighted and defiant laugh while incapacitated with what could have been yet another recurrence of the Great Plague that had devastated England in her childhood. There was ample evidence of evil in her time, and there is ample evidence of "the Fiend" in my own time—miseries and evil machinations over which to weep and to rage. Julian received the courage to resist, to defy, and to laugh.

This book is about Julian's defiant laughter, in her own words and from her own time, and my teaching these words in historical context

---

1. I use the Penguin edition of *Revelations of Divine Love* (1998), which provides a translation from Julian's Middle English into everyday modern English by Elizabeth Spearing. I will note first whether the quote is from the ST (Short Text) or LT (Long Text), followed by chapter number (which will allow you to locate a reference if you are using a different edition) and page number in the Penguin volume.

to other people confounded by life. Like many women I know, I find it almost impossible to laugh while in full awareness of evil. As part of my vocation, I teach and write about war, torture, drone strikes, sexual domination, and racial terror. Evil makes me angry, scared, and sad. I laugh from my centered, most courageous part of my soul, a part of myself that I can access only when in the presence of people whom I trust with my full, vulnerable truth and hope. Then, and only then, I sometimes laugh so loudly that strangers turn around and stare. I snort and spontaneously clap, sometimes with my hands in the air praising God for whatever truth I have just heard. I have come to experience this full-on laughter as a miracle—as a dose of sanity to help me move on to another day, to face more of the bloody truths of my own time.

Nicki Minaj is a musician to whose music my daughters and I dance in the car. Her songs feature a laugh that is all-out courageous and joyful, rebellious and delighted. She turns around and looks squarely at the punishing music industry and laughs, with a snort. When I first heard the laughter in Nicki Minaj's music, it struck me that her combination of courage and elation was like the laugh Julian laughed in the face of the Devil. Her lyrics mock the ways a male-dominated and racist music industry measures women's bodies, and she plays with caricatures of sexuality, making them powerfully her own. With defiant indecorum, she laughs. Julian also faced full-on many bloody truths about power and cruelty, and she refused to flinch.

Sometime around 1373, when Julian was about thirty years old, she received a series of visions as an answer to prayer. She asks for "vivid perception of Christ's Passion," meaning Jesus's death on a cross. By "Passion," Julian means a particular kind of passion. She asks to be infused with a full sense of Jesus when, by her theology, Jesus was bringing all of the world into God. That is, Julian asks to be one with Jesus on the cross. (I will explain this more below.) She also asks for "bodily sickness." And she asks for "three wounds" (ST: 1, 3). Today this may sound bizarre. At first reading it sounded masochistic to me. But it was not odd during the Middle Ages for fervent Christians to ask God for Jesus to become one with their own body. It was not strange for people seeking holiness to feel in their bones a union with Jesus on the cross. Julian interprets her time of sickness as a gift of vision from God. In her room, focusing on a simple household crucifix on the wall, she sees everyone and everything that ever was and ever will be held safe by God in love.

When I say Julian laughed at evil, I mean she asked God to be with her while she kept looking the Fiend in the eye, knowing that, as she puts it, she had been given "strength to resist all the fiends of hell and all spiritual enemies" (ST: 3, 7). Rather than viewing the world around her as filled to the brim with misery, she saw simple miracles and resilient safety. She did not deny that there was a fiend to be conquered. She did not pretend the world was simple. The Devil is no-thing, but that does not mean Julian denied the evil around her. Because of this her laughter is all the more powerful an antidote to a religion of fear.

Julian received suffering as a kind of inoculation against dread. A reasonable response to the manifold traumas around her—recurring plague, famine, a brutal aristocracy—would have been precisely to catch a contagion of terror. Instead she changed the whole scene. In her vision God gave her the blood of Jesus, straight from Jesus's own body, in a way that changed how she saw the entire universe, including God. Seeing God's "familiar love," she knew God as "hanging about us in tender love," like "our clothing" (ST: 3, 7). Hers is not the only way to understand and live the Christian faith, but she has helped to shape my life and the lives of many other people seeking truth. I am still trying to follow her lead—dancing, laughing, seeing, crying, and thinking, thinking, thinking, and, again . . . praying and remembering how to trust enough to laugh from the most centered part of my body and soul.

I teach Ethics (capital E) at a prestigious secular university, where an ethicist worth her salt cannot offer dressed-up academic platitudes about what is ethically wholesome or what is ethically legal or what is considered moral to some universal judge of clean living. I cannot evade the hardest questions about the world around me or about Jesus. If I do not ask a bewildering question about ethics and God, students will call me out as giving too simple an account of their world. I am also a mother. Both of my daughters live with the stigma of a "broken home," a phrase that is still used in North Carolina by both older and young adults who grew up with a simple vision of wholeness. The brokenness my daughters knew before our home was publicly, officially "broken" has left me with recurrent questions about the possibility of love. Julian's writings have helped me not to give up on either the most unbearable sorts of truths or on Jesus as truth. Julian has helped me listen to the hardest questions coming at me and the most painful questions coming from within me. During times that have seemed to me and to many other people around me to be nothing short of apocalyptic, Julian has helped me resist running away from reality.

I came to Julian by accident. You may be reading this book because you already love Julian of Norwich. I first read her *Revelations of Divine Love* in a hurry, and with impatience. It was 1999, and I had just started my position as a new teacher. I was teaching a large Introduction to Christian Ethics class at Duke Divinity School, and I did not have a single woman on the list of readings from "the classics." A colleague suggested Julian of Norwich. When I looked puzzled, he said something like, "You know her. She wrote 'All shall be well, all shall be well, all manner of things shall be well'?" No. I'd never heard of her, and she sounded stupid.

"All shall be well"? I had heard too many Christians say some version of "All things work for good for those who endure misery" to people who needed a friend just to sit with them in silence. I had also seen "All is well" language used like a Jedi mind trick on people who were aggrieved and grieving. "All is well," and God knows what is good, so what you are grieving or raging against is not worth all of those tears or all that rage. No, thank you. I had heard this language before. No more of that soporific crap for me. But Julian's name kept coming up as a crucial theologian to read and to teach.

I read *Revelations of Divine Love* while trying hard to perform openness and grace for those around me at work and in my new hometown. This, while I was trying to convey a message of joy in the midst of chaos. That chaos was, in fact, a recurrence of abuse in my own home. In this state of intimidation, scrutiny, and almost unbearable fragility, Julian became my lodestar. She was my focal point as I tried to twirl with a semblance of grace on the stage of my life. This book is in part a testimony to how the visions of a courageous woman can transform a setting of dread into a call to courage. "All shall be well" became, for me, a refusal of intimidation, scrutiny, and shame. Julian helped me to look at even the most terrifying truth of my own personal life and trust in the love of God.

I have found that Julian's visions resonate even with readers who have not grown up Christian. Her words about hope and love can speak to people who are privy to secular messages of despair, despondency, competition, and straight-up hate. Images in *Better Homes and Gardens* recommend ways to have, well, *better* homes and gardens. *Cosmopolitan* offers unique tricks to make sure a woman is not alone, or disappointing, on a Saturday night. *Men's Health* shows men how to achieve a configuration on their abdominals known as a "six-pack" while also advising them how to choose the best craft beer. Television viewers in the United States view high-end fights for survival and fitness on *The Sopranos* or *Game of Thrones* and, even more popular, literal fights for scarce goods on *The Price Is Right* and "fight nights" promoted by Ultimate Fighting Championship. Julian has helped me to diagnose and counter such subtle and overt calls to see the world as a competition for scarce resources.

For some Christian readers, her visions powerfully counter a particular form of Christian faith that manipulates anxiety to quicken obedience and compliance. This medieval anchorite, writing with courage when Christianity and political hierarchy were intertwined to convince people to shut up and stay in their place, can speak across centuries to embolden Christians who have been privy to a similarly toxic blend of religion and politics. Writers and speakers in the United States continue to use Christian language to intimidate and to shame. Julian's visions offer a hearty rebuttal of this use for Christians and for non-Christians who must navigate a political scene where Christian language is used to scare people. Preachers showcased by major media outlets too often speak a false gospel of obedience and order, an isolating message of individual responsibility, or some combination of the two. Commentators like the *New York Times* columnist David Brooks reinforce these messages, diagnosing humanity as inherently narcissistic and prescribing selflessness for everyone, as if prescribing fluoride in water.

Julian saw visions of Jesus's blood coming to her and for her, with no intermediary, during the same decade when, customarily, only priests received the cup of blessing (the blood) and the bread (or body) was parceled out according to a strict division of who was above whom in an aristocratic, feudal system. Her resultant laughter is a testimony today against a summons to purifying humiliation and obedience. Julian's visions of God's familiarity and love counter messages of austerity and obeisance to hierarchical ordering. And she wrote with an intention of being read, by real people, from a position of kinship rather than superiority.

Nicholas Watson and Jacqueline Jenkins (2006) edited a volume on Julian that provides her original writings, in Middle English, and copious notes on the particular words and historical context of her writings. In their introduction to the volume they write, "*A Revelation* [meaning the Long Text] is a work with no real precedent: a speculative vernacular theology, not modeled on earlier texts but structured as a prolonged investigation into the divine, whose prophetic goal is to birth a new understanding of human living into the world and of the nature of God in his interactions with the world, not just for theologians but for everyone" (3). What they mean by "a speculative vernacular theology" is this: Julian was willing to ask questions that a woman was not supposed to ask. In fact only men trained in theology at Oxford or Cambridge University were considered qualified to ask the questions she asked. Julian was "speculative" in that she speculated—she asked questions. And she wrote in the vernacular, meaning she wrote in English, the language people not trained at Oxford or Cambridge spoke to one another about everyday things. Julian was a churchwoman and a prophet who wanted people to catch sight of what she saw and to become curious about what it meant that God told her that God's meaning is, always and for eternity, love. She wanted people to think, see, sorrow, and *laugh at the Devil* with her. This is my invitation, in my own vernacular, to join in this vision.

ACKNOWLEDGMENTS

Miriam Angress has edited a book that crosses boundaries. I am grateful for her courage. I am grateful to Judith Hoover and Liz Smith for correcting and clarifying my prose. Elizabeth Spearing translated Julian of Norwich from Julian's English to my own. I am grateful for her expertise. Shannon Gayk told me reading Julian is important. Professor Gayk also recommended more readings about vernacular theology. Elizabeth Spearing and Shannon Gayk prompted me to ask librarians at Duke University for more essays about this period. I am grateful to every librarian at Duke who made this book possible. Elizabeth Benson, Judith Heyhoe, and David Lott read the manuscript and helped me to write in the vernacular. Mariya Paykova Tivnan taught me the difference. Liturgy does not respect boundaries of past and present. David Lott read the manuscript and helped me convey the present and past of liturgy. Students at Duke Divinity School, University of Virginia, Point Loma, and Princeton Seminary helped me discern how best to teach Julian. Robert C. Lyons wrote a close reading of Julian in 2000 that helped me decide to teach her works as long as I have words to speak. Silas Barber and Amanda Smith listened as I sorted out what most matters. Lillian Daniel and J. Kameron Carter reminded me to preach. Rachel and Emily inspire every word I write. I now dedicate this book to my parents. This is long overdue. Dear

Carol Tisdale Hall and Robert Edward Hall, I love you. You were my mom and dad. You are now Cookie and Pop to Emily, Rachel, and my beloved nephews. You taught me to read words closely, to love real people, to be brave, to sing hymns even when I do not have the spirit in me, and always to risk the truth.

INTRODUCTION
Love in Everything

Though the three persons of the Trinity are all equal in
themselves, my soul understood love most clearly, yes, and
God wants us to consider and enjoy love in everything. And
this is the knowledge of which we are most ignorant; for
some of us believe that God is all mighty and has power
to do everything, and that he has wisdom and knows how
to do everything, but that he is all love and is willing to do
everything—there we stop.

—JULIAN OF NORWICH, *Revelations of Divine Love*

I have tried to think past the "stop" that Julian of Norwich writes
about in this passage. I have always found it almost impossible truly
to believe in my bones and my flesh and my brain that God is "all love"
and truly "all love" *for me*.

Omnipotent? Yes. God is *omni* (all) *potent* (powerful).

Omniscient? Yes. God is *omni* (all) *scient* (wise).

I know these two attributes make God God. I was taught this in
Sunday school when I was a child. Summer after summer I sang of
this in hymns during worship at church camp. In between listening
to the 1980s rock group Van Halen on my cassette player, I had mem-
orized the hymn "Immortal, Invisible, God Only Wise!" God knows

everything, and God can do everything. Check and check. I say these affirmations by rote.

But omni-loving?

I am not alone in this doubt.

One of the earliest examples we have of someone reading Julian of Norwich is in the record of a nun named Margaret Gascoigne, from seventeenth-century France. That was a long time ago, but Sister Margaret is not so far away. Margaret was writing about her struggles to believe that Jesus was actually *for her*. She was trying to believe in Jesus in a way that was more than just a required affirmation to which she said YES in order to be allowed into heaven. Margaret focused on a passage by Julian to help center herself. The passage Sister Margaret focused on is translated from Middle English in this way (God speaking): "Consider me alone my precious child, make me your object, I am *enough for you*" (LT: 36, 92). As Nicholas Watson and Jacqueline Jenkins (2006, 15) put it, Julian's vision "speaks words of comfort across two and a half centuries to a dying woman still beset by the uncertainties of a theologically gloomier age."

Gloomy is a more polite word than I would use. But the word *gloomy* begins to tell the truth of a doubt that I have had and that others have also had for centuries. If God is all-knowing and all-powerful—if both of these statements are true—then God may also be omni-cruel. Or, if God "loves," then God's love is twisted. God is the creepiest, most calculating, most omni-patient sort of horribly cold lover. Is God the sort of supposedly loving lover who waits until the very end of all time to reassure people whom he supposedly loves that love is truly love?

Julian of Norwich sees that God is all love and is willing to do everything. For us. For me. For you. And that "is" truly is an "is," not a "will be" or a "was." Her vision is love, and love now. Her vision is not about a love-pie in the sky. This vision is not insipid, but it is also so complicated that it took her many years to describe what she had seen.

This book is my cerebral and soul-wracked reckoning with the possibility that Julian of Norwich saw the truth about God. In four parts I sift through things I have learned and the questions I still have:

Time: what it means that Julian says God is willing to do everything, present tense.

Truth: what it means that Christians know a truth that makes us odd.

Blood:[1] what difference it makes for us that Jesus was bloody and comes to us in the blood of Holy Communion.

Bodies: how you and I are a blood-and-bone miracle held by God.

I cannot tell my story of reading her without a short history lesson. This part matters for how Julian thinks about our matter. At the beginning of her Short Text she writes, "I asked for three graces of God's gift. The first was vivid perception of Christ's Passion, the second was bodily sickness and the third was for God to give me three wounds. I thought of the first as I was meditating: it seemed to me that I could feel the Passion of Christ strongly, but yet I longed by God's grace to feel it more intensely" (ST: 1, 3). By praying to come right up next to Jesus and "feel the Passion of Christ strongly," Julian may have created and received her own opiate, dulling the pain around her with bloody hallucinations. Some readers have decided that is exactly what she did.

A woman, a visionary, a universalist, a writer from a long time ago: Julian of Norwich is by many different categories easy to dismiss. I gave a lecture about Julian at a local church, and a stately priest, already extra-stately in his clerical robe, stood at the back of the lecture hall and asked me about Julian's "mental illness." He explained in front of the members of his congregation that he had been taught in seminary that Julian was put into "solitary confinement" after having a "mental breakdown." I have not heard or read an actual scholar

---

1. Different Christian groups use different terms for what happens when people receive a bit of bread and a bit of squashed grapes (whether wine or Welch's) during worship. There are good reasons for calling this practice by particular names, but I am going to use the common terms interchangeably. For the purposes of my book, the Lord's Supper, Communion, the Mass, and the Eucharist are the same. If you do not believe that Jesus is present in some material way in the practice of receiving a bit of bread and squashed grapes, I hope this book is still useful to you.

of medieval history call Julian "hysterical," but she has been given that loaded label over the centuries by men and women who have not known how to think through what she saw. Taken apart in little quotations, she can seem trite. Her history, taken apart for a case study, may make her appear odd. Her theological affirmations were so dangerous it is a miracle she was not executed. In order to catch sight of the truthful courage and beauty of her visions, it is important to know about the theology of her time and about the meaning of her eventual position as an anchorite.

The name that Julian's mother gave her is not available. Julian was not part of the people in the England of her time to be recorded for posterity. She was not of the aristocracy. We cannot look up the name she went by before she came to be called Julian of Norwich. We refer to her by that name because she eventually became an anchorite, named after her church. Anchorites were a diverse group, but they had one thing in common: they were anchored to a particular church; at some point they each dedicated their full-time existence to living in a small apartment attached to a church.

We know from official records that, by 1393, Julian had become an anchorite in the busy city of Norwich, at the busy church of St. Julian's, a name it received centuries before her birth. Sometime in the late fourteenth century, this writer we now know as Julian took the name of that church. We also know from historical records that she was sought out as a sage. So while some anchorites were secluded, it is likely Julian was at least periodically busy. To think of her as being in solitary confinement is absurd. Catherynne M. Valente, a fantasy and science-fiction writer who loves Julian and writes a blog about spirituality, describes the life of an anchorite this way: "She is an oracle, an academic, a hermit in the midst of life." As an anchorite in a busy church in a busy city, Julian would have been very much "in the midst of life." People might have come to hear her words after seeing a beheading or after having buried a husband or after having been accused of heresy.

St. Julian's Church was not named for Julian of Norwich. She was named for the church. But Julian's Church in Norwich may still be around because of her. The woman we now know as Julian of Norwich loved that church, and she became a part of it. St. Julian's Church was bombed almost to the ground by orders of a German general during World War II, and the church was rebuilt because many people read and loved Julian of Norwich. Tourists who know nothing about the second-century St. Julian, a man for whom the church was originally named, go to Norwich because they believe Julian of Norwich was holy. Pilgrims hope to see the church to which she was attached. Some take Holy Communion there. Maybe they hope to feel close to her laughter.

Julian was a visionary. Around the time that her words were circulating, people were also threatened, imprisoned, and tortured as examples of how not to see the world. King Henry IV and his parliament passed a statute in 1401 called *De heretico comburendo*. The statute ordered any person adhering to heretical views to be "publicly burnt in a high place." The document added, "May punishment of this sort strike fear into the minds of others" (Given-Wilson et al. 2005). Today a pub in Norwich bears the name Lollards Pit, and its sign hanging out front features naked people in flames. The notion that an English leader would be so intertwined with a form of faith as to decree death for anyone who thought off-brand is now peculiar enough to be a pub's advertising gimmick. At the turn of the fourteenth to the fifteenth century, when Julian was writing, the king and the archbishop of Canterbury were all up in one another's business. When they were not fighting against one another, they were reinforcing their own power with every intertwined form of control they had available. The century during which Julian received her visions and wrote her words culminated in a royal decree to regulate who was allowed to write and speak about God.

The turn of the fourteenth to the fifteenth century was a time of holy mischief. People who were literally hungry due to wheat shortages and feudal machinations were also hungry to read Scripture in their own language, to hold a scrap of scriptural verse in their hands. It was a time riddled with despair and sadistic repression. Julian wrote with temerity at this intersection. It is one of the reasons people return to her words, and to the church now known for her name. It is a reason

I turn to her—in order to look the ugly truth in the eye and not only refuse to flinch but "to consider and enjoy love in everything." Julian's Norwich was not so different from any postdisaster, postapocalyptic human world in Western history. She was about eight years old when a horrific plague, known at the time as "the Great Plague," spread from Europe and the Middle East to England, killing half of the people in many towns and creating a sense of impending disaster that reverberated for generations, through recurrence in England of the deadly disease itself and in graphic memories of loved ones lost. She was seeing visions of Jesus's blood coming to her and for her, with no intermediary, during the same decade when, customarily, only priests received the cup of blessing (the blood) and the bread (or body) was parceled out according to a strict division of who was superior to whom. With peasant uprisings throughout England, the rules that governed a system of feudalism were being challenged and violently reinforced.

Under English feudalism, rules about who could speak to whom were kept in part by memorizing who was whose child, by class-based rules about clothing, and by which language people spoke. If you spoke Latin, you were trained in theology and could talk about God. If you spoke French, you were part of the aristocracy. And if you spoke English, you were someone who mostly did not matter to the first two groups, unless you tried to change things. Then you were punished. Frederick Christian Bauerschmidt (1999, 22) quotes the historian R. H. Tawney on this point: "The gross facts of the social order are accepted in all their harshness and brutality. They are accepted with astonishing docility, and, except on rare occasions, there is no question of reconstruction." Bauerschmidt explains, "This 'harshness and brutality' is accepted as intrinsic to the social order" (22).

Julian's Long Text was written at a time of societal and personal crisis. Common sense included also a dose of death. The dread of death may have been just a whiff if you were among the few people who lived above the fray. But it was palpable if you were a starving peasant or a commoner who wanted to talk about Scripture or changes to the feudal system or if your village had a recurrence of plague. Part of what I found fascinating even the first time I read Julian is how, as Bauerschmidt (1999, 14) puts it, hers is "a particularly crucial period of transition." The "docility" that Tawney describes in his writings on medieval England is accurate. But there was resistance. I have come to read Julian right at the juncture of dread, docility, rebellion, and hope. In the mix of all of this, Julian received visions of love, love, and more love. These visions left her asking complex questions for, as she tells us, "fifteen years and more" about the meaning of what she had seen. The answer she received, after praying on her visions, is clear. The answer she received from God verges on bossy. She writes, "My spiritual understanding received an answer, which was this": "Do you want to know what your Lord meant? Know well that love was what he meant. Who showed you this? Love. What did he show? Love. Why did he show it to you? For love. Hold fast to this and you will know and understand more of the same; but you will never understand or know from it anything else for all eternity" (LT: 86, 179). She continues, "I saw quite certainly in this and in everything that God loved us before he made us; and his love has never diminished and never shall" (LT: 86, 179). The last few pages of Julian's book about her visions leave us knowing Love, Love, Love, and Love. And, by the way, focusing on these visions of Love will, with grace, lead us back into an answer of Love. If you want from her visions a different answer to a different question than the ones she is asking, and if you crave a different answer than the one she received, she warns you that you can go ahead and look for "all eternity" at her writings and not find what you are looking for. Bauerschmidt (1999, 160) writes that, for Julian, "From creation to consummation in heavenly bliss, God sees all of humanity as enfolded within the humanity of Christ." Focusing on the cross, Julian returns again and again to see in Jesus Christ God's vision of love.

John Piper is a popular Christian writer and speaker in the United States. He gave a short lecture in 2009 to the annual meeting of the

Religious Newswriters Association about a movement and marketing scheme he calls "the New Calvinists."[2] In his summary of the basic message of New Calvinism, the most important contribution is its emphasis on human "insignificance." Using examples from a syndicated cartoon and a granola advertisement, Piper suggested to the gathered reporters that there is a deep longing among people in the United States for an authoritative word about God's power, particularly after September 11, 2001. As Piper describes it, people desire the truth that God is omnipotent and that, in contrast, humans and our bodies and daily concerns are like dust. When faced with an unimaginable tragedy like September 11, what people most want is an affirmation that God controls everything and mere human beings control nothing.

As I write this book, the New Calvinists often still proclaim this, what I call a Gospel of Austerity, to generations of Christians and seekers who are trying to live with the aftermath of two wars, during an economic debacle, hearing about drone strikes in Pakistan, dealing with the militarization of police in cities across the country, and learning about torture in prisons from Chicago to Cuba. It is fair to characterize the neo-Calvinist message Piper summarized this way: If you are still alive in this age of terror, thank God, and stop whining about government surveillance. If you still have any job of any kind during this, the Second Great Depression, pick up your broom, and stop complaining about minimum wage. Oh, and keep going to church every Sunday, because God deserves your obeisance.

Julian of Norwich was a woman living through the tumultuous Middle Ages in England, and she saw things differently. She asked a different sort of question, and she embodied a different answer. She assumed that God is all-powerful. She also assumed God's knowledge of all that is. She didn't have to underscore God's knowledge by making sure everyone knows human beings are senseless. Her primary ques-

---

2. There are different ways to read any theologian in the Christian tradition, and John Calvin has been read in different ways over the centuries. Piper was speaking about a particular way of using some of Calvin's words today.

tion was about God's love. The query that kept her going back again and again and again to the cross concerned neither God's omnipotence nor God's omniscience. Her query concerned God's *omniamity*.[3]

In her decades of writing and rewriting her one book, Julian returns to Jesus Christ on the cross like a dancer uses a focal point. When twirling in a circle, a dancer fixes on a point to steady his balance and to avoid keeling over. Julian did the same with the image of Jesus on the cross. She uses a metaphor of a toddler who, when faced with danger, runs to her "mother's bosom." Christians seek the "Lord's breast" in this way (LT: 74, 164). Using maternal language for God does not mean that Julian softens the real monsters of her world. Plagues, public hangings, forms of domination subtle and overt in a drastically hierarchical country infused with Christianity—these were not figments of a fearful toddler's nightmares. These cruelties were the bloody truth. But Jesus is also the truth. Seeing the world truthfully through Jesus is her task. Jesus is the reason Julian is able to see the microfissures and gaping ramifications of evil and go past the "stop" of doubt in God's omniamity. God is "all love and is willing to do everything." That is our focal point, our mother's bosom, our question and our answer.

You may have had or may eventually have your own particular snowflake-of-arsenic difficulties and social torments that lead you to doubt or scorn God's omniamity. Divorce, death, war, domestic violence, cancer, bullying at work or at school, imprisonment—personal horror is unique, poisonous in a way that is singular and almost indescribable to another person. I do not presume to interpret Julian authoritatively for everyone. I write alongside Julian, in a personal, sometimes pastoral, and unapologetically political way. I assume that all research is in some way introspective. I also assume that my own body is related to the politics of what we might call the "social" body. The rules of how I am supposed to think about God and God's relation to me are related to the rules of how I dress, what words I can and cannot say, how I am supposed to raise my daughters, and so forth. Any

3. This is a word I made up. "Omni" means all, and "amity" means love.

close, careful reading I give of a treasured book is also formed by my reading of myself and the politics around me.

I should say a word up front about that most contested p word, *political*. The first book I read about Julian, back when I was preparing my class lectures on *Revelations of Divine Love*, was Bauerschmidt's (1999). Without the telescope of his historical interpretation, she would have remained at the periphery of my spiritual universe. The name of his book is *Julian of Norwich and the Mystical Body Politic of Christ*, and the ways that England was politically fraught during Julian's time is a central part of his analysis. I was persuaded quickly, reading Julian herself, that she was not vapid. But I might have missed the political import of her piety if I had not also read Bauerschmidt's book on the *body politic of Christ*. He described for me in detail the context for Julian's visions of safety in the cross.

Having taught Julian now for over fifteen years, I have decided that to read her without attention to her politics risks turning her *Revelations* into a logic puzzle. An apolitical reading may become a bloodless interpretation of a book that is often about blood. A comparison to another female writer might help. Nadine Gordimer was a novelist writing during apartheid in South Africa, and she was criticized, threatened, and censored for being too "political" in her stories. Gordimer countered that, under a regime that defined every waking moment by procedures of racial and ethnic exclusion and division, human interaction was ineluctably political. In her own time Julian saw copious blood flowing from the cross that "kinned" people who were by law supposed to remain unkinned. That is, she saw people made into equals and relatives who were not supposed to be kin with one another.

At the turn of the fourteenth to the fifteenth century, England was divided into social stations even more rigidly than it is currently. The term *blue blood* was not a joke; as during other times and in other places, the sense that some people had superior blood and others had inferior blood was based in what I might call (somewhat ironically) "common" sense. And the things that went on under the label "Jesus Christ" or "Church" were part of that hierarchical ordering. Bauerschmidt (1999, 18–20) describes the historical record from this period in a way that takes time to understand, but it is worth that time: "The celebration of the mass, particularly the High Mass, in which the priest was assisted by a deacon, subdeacon, and clerks, was a complex rite that depended on the participants properly performing their distinct functions." He continues, "This hierarchical nature of the rite was vividly expressed in the way that subdeacon, deacon, and the priest were ranged on increasingly higher steps before the altar, as well as the complex order of precedence in which the choir was censed and the Gospel book kissed." The way Holy Communion was arranged reinforced the order of people in England at that time. Holy Communion was like a pageant of the different ranks of people, and it was not the case that the first went last and the last went first. The first layer of people even argued with one another, during celebrations of Holy Communion, about who was first among the first. At the time that Julian laughed at the Devil, there also was a practice called the "ceremonial kissing of the paxbread." Bauerschmidt relates a story of a man intent on being higher in the ordering of the first sorts of people who used the paxbread (peace bread) to hit the person carrying the paxbread, angry that someone else had established prominence by kissing the bread before he did.

These practices were all tangled up with ways that the English aristocracy and the Roman Catholic Church were attempting to keep the lid on changes to the system of Christianity. People in the upper ranks of England during Julian's time argued and threatened one another over who could be at the front of the line to kiss Jesus. Let that historical fact sink in. I cannot now unsee what Bauerschmidt helped me to see. I cannot take the politics back out of Julian's visions, given what I now know. So my book on Julian is also political. Her visions of Jesus's blood coming to her and of Jesus's blood making each one of us family are politically loaded.

There is another escape route away from reading Julian politically. In his book on this period in England's history, *Richard Rolle and the Invention of Authority*, Nicholas Watson (1991) helpfully explains how thinkers thinking alongside Julian can render her hygienically apolitical by tossing her into the stratosphere and leaving her there. People may be tempted to hagiography when reading a writer who has seen visions from God, "approaching the verbal surface of a text with a mixture of aesthetic and religious awe" (Watson 1991, 2). *Hagiography* technically means writings about a saint. Writing hagiography today, in my world, means turning a merely human writer into an angel. I am using the term to describe the way some writers make another writer into someone who is not writing for flawed people like me. Julian might become worthy of my awe and my study, but, with this sort of hagiographic misreading, I myself become unworthy of reading her as writing *for me*.

It does not help us that someone at Penguin Books decided to put on the cover of their edition, which contains the best translation, a young woman who is *not* Julian of Norwich. Roger van der Weyden's *Portrait of a Young Woman Wearing a Coif* presents a person in a starched, clean, white coif, looking like she might, possibly, sometimes smile but would never laugh at the Devil and probably would not risk the indecorum of laughing like Nicki Minaj. Although women who were not in a religious order wore coifs during Julian's time, the connotation for readers today is of a prim nun. The way the book's cover is situated, the words "Penguin Classics" and "Julian of Norwich: Revelations of Divine Love" also cover the woman's ample breasts and folded, ungloved hands. (You have to turn the book over for the full view of the chosen painting.)

Watson's funniest example of the silly "Blessed Mother Julian" reading that leaves her floating angelically above worldly politics is this: "What Mother Julian meant we cannot know in this life." Hogwash, Watson says. (He does not actually use the word *hogwash*, but it fits.) He recommends a way of avoiding such silliness when reading Julian: "Focus instead on what we can call a mystical writer's 'predicament' in formulating doctrinal positions, articulating an appropriately didactic discourse and describing mystical experience. . . . Look at the specifically *mundane* pressures that beset a mystical text, impelling it toward complex and ambiguous claims for its own status as an embodiment of truth" (1991, 2). In other words, think about this "mystical text" with the actual earth in mind.

Given that Watson is a medievalist and he has gone to the trouble of italicizing the word *mundane* in his book, I looked up the uses of *mundane* during Julian's time. Then as now, it means earthly, earthy, of this real planet we walk around on and sleep on and eat from. Watson is explaining to his own readers that it makes sense to read a writer like Julian as a person who was writing from a particular real life that involved "pressures" that are right here, on this ground, held by the same gravity that holds us today. Your "predicaments" will be unique, but to read Julian as a non-earth creature is to avoid not only her earthly challenges but your own. Her claims to truth are "complex and ambiguous," Watson notes, but that may make her writing all the more fascinating as an "embodiment of truth." I am not interested in teaching a Christian writer who is cocksure. A mundane theologian who was confused periodically and who needed time to sort and sift and think and pray in order to write down what she learned from God is worth my trouble.

Van der Weyden's *Portrait of a Young Woman Wearing a Coif* does suit Julian in one respect. Her eyes hint that she has much more to say than you would at first glance guess. Her eyes look a bit like Mona Lisa's eyes. Teaching Julian has been different from teaching someone in the Christian Tradition (with a capital T) who bears the authoritative stamp of Gravitas (with a capital G). Julian is a woman who wrote like a woman, and she wrote about blood. The challenge of convincing young, conservative students who have been told to trust only theologians with penises to pick up her book and read it has been a surprising gift. It is precisely the "mundane" particulars and her "predicament" that hooks them to read her visions as more than a task to check off their list. Reading her politically has helped students not to underestimate the more that is hinted at by the painting on the cover of the book. Julian's vision of God's omniamity in the "plentiful shedding of his precious blood" is a different perspective on the world than that of the various John Pipers of her own time, men determined to shore up God's sovereignty and accentuate human impotence (ST: 5, 9). The mundane aspects of Norwich life six hundred years ago help me to see and to teach Julian's visions of God's "homely" friendship with crimson vitality.

Here is one basic, mundane intersection of Julian's visions and what goes on in a church worship service today. Christians are supposed to believe that the people gathered in worship are Jesus's body on earth and that the bread on the altar is Jesus's body for our bodies. So how the food line at church is structured matters for how people see one another. Julian prayed to receive Jesus and saw each person as part of the same body of Jesus. She saw a Jesus who did not parcel out himself according to the strict hierarchy of England, but who was grace itself, in bodily form and also in his body. Jesus is profligate grace, giving life and making each human life real and good and family with all others.

That blurring of lines between groups of people was a capital offense by the fifteenth century. Julian of Norwich could have been hanged for describing the holy miscegenation she had received in her visions. This may explain her frequent use of *maybe* and *like* and *perhaps* and other words that have marked Julian as "feminine" over the centuries. (I have had students dismiss Julian outright because *Revelations of Divine Love* does not read like a debate or as an academic duel.) She saw people who supposedly had different kinds of blood all mixed together in Jesus's blood and knit together in Jesus's body. It took Julian repeated, careful engagement with what she knew was the official doctrine of Holy Church and what she knew she had seen from God to land on the strong possibility of universalism in the final version of her Long Text. Her use of what may be seen as tentative language could be in part her deference to Church authorities, but this language also represents her persistence to find the best words to express the challenging truths she had received in her initial visions.

The Lollards, after whom the trendy Norwich pub I mentioned is named, has become a catch-all term for heretics sufficiently troublesome to be censored or killed. The term was used most frequently for followers of John Wycliffe, who argued for the translation of Scripture into the language most people actually used to communicate: English. Many of the people labeled "Lollards" thought Christians ought to be able to hear the words used by another person in worship in their own language and to hear Scripture read by another person in words they could understand. Again, at this time in England the royalty spoke and wrote in French, and holy people in charge wrote and spoke in Latin. The language of Christianity at Julian's time was regimented to keep the social body—that is, the people who made up the daily life of reality—divided into layers. There were those allowed to read the holy words, handle the holy objects, and be buried in the holiest places, and those who were not. And, again, there were gradations among the various layers. To be anachronistic to make a point, the lords and ladies went before the ladies and gentlemen went before the doctors and lawyers went before the hotel heiresses and heirs went before the extended family of a once celebrated athlete went before the common people who ride the bus because they can't afford gas, and so on. Can you imagine if you walked into a church that required people to line up for the Lord's Supper that way? Can you imagine being told you could not talk about theology until you learned Latin? Or that you had no right to learn French because your blood was not the right sort of blood?

The historic fact of the plague is also important for understanding Julian's visions. Grace Jantzen (1988, 8) has a summary of the human misery and Church crisis brought on by the Great Plague that I cannot summarize better than I can quote:

People died, horribly and suddenly and in great numbers. It was so contagious that one contemporary witness describes how anyone who touched the sick or the dead immediately caught the disease and died himself, so that priests who ministered to the dying were flung into the same grave with their penitents. It was impossible for the clergy to keep up with all those who required last rites, and to die unshriven was seen as a catastrophe of eternal proportions. Nor could the people who died be buried with dignity. . . . The psychological impact on the survivors was incalculable, made worse in subsequent years by the further outbreaks which occurred at unpredictable intervals.

Jantzen explains that more than a third of the people of Norwich died during this relatively short period of time, and around half of the priests died. One word in the quote that was new to me when I first read it years ago is *unshriven*. Priests who did not flee the deadly plague were dying, and so their parishioners were dying without being given the last rites—the prayers and actions performed by a priest to give those at the end of life a chance to confess and to receive Communion, or the Mass, before they died. Jantzen points out that people were not only losing their loved ones left and right; they understood that they were losing their loved ones in a way that would separate them forever from one another. People were dying without receiving the practice that secured one's hope for eternal life with God and one another. So during a time when food shortages periodically swept through England and there was not enough bread for people to eat, there was a spiritual crisis as well; people not only died of the plague, but they died in a way that left survivors in despair. Julian grew up in the wake of this tragedy.

Piper argued that the mass murder of September 11 brought on a crisis of biblical proportions, eliciting in people a desire to be reminded of their own submission and insignificance before the Lord God Almighty and his inscrutable purposes. There is an unhelpful way to point to 9/11 as the cause of every ensuing cultural impulse in the United States, and I understand it is possible to overestimate the import of 9/11, but I have found reading Julian of Norwich helpful for thinking about different responses to what might be called collective trauma, or trauma suffered at a societal level by a large group of people. I have come to believe that it is not merely coincidence that there has been an outbreak of medievalphilia in the United States since 9/11. I interpret the popularity of movies like the *Lord of the Rings* trilogy and the television show *Game of Thrones* as a misdirected desire on the part of viewers to watch staged hangings, beheadings, impalings, sexual violation, and large-scale destruction to experience a manageable form of affliction. The rise in violence on screen (large and small screen) after 9/11 may be similar to the impulse of a survivor of sexual violence to cut herself in order to try to become the master of the pain she has endured.

During a time of misery and division, Julian asked to receive a bodily experience of Jesus's suffering. By one reading, this was nuts. I think her request for proximity to pain was a way of responding to the manifold traumas going on in her time. I think she asked for the wounds of Jesus to take her away from a cycle of despair, shame, domination, and the violence of retribution that tempts at least some people during times of political tumult.

Julian's answer of God's omniamity is a redirection away from an obsessive rotation of fear, shame, domination, and submission. Her visions of God's love scramble the hierarchical ordering of things. Or, to put it differently, all bloodlines are bled together. And her visions answer that God has not favored the survivors over the afflicted. Her answer to the crises of her time was not to reinforce the order of things, affirm the rightness of authority, and threaten other people subtly or overtly with God's wrath or God's indifference.

On 9/11/01 children across the United States watched their parents and their teachers watching their televisions with horror as people died in ways that are unthinkable. One response to seeing human beings reduced to worse than nothingness is to submit to and inhabit that version of religious truth. We are dust; deal with it. Another response, Julian's response, is, eventually, after years of trying to understand what she had received from God, to discern a vision of redemption:

> At one time our good Lord said, "All manner of things shall be well"; and at another time he said, "You shall see for yourself that all manner of things shall be well"; and the soul understood

these two sayings differently. On the one hand he wants us to know that he does not only concern himself with great and noble things, but also with small, humble, and simple things, with both one and the other; and this is what he means when he says, "All manner of things shall be well": for he wants us to know that the smallest things shall not be forgotten. (LT: 32)

By the proper, analytically true reckoning of her time, a significant percentage of the population were eternally lost. By the proper, political reckoning of her time the great and noble were the arbiters to restore proper order and win again God's favor. I am willing to wager that the proper, commonsense reckoning of many Christians during Julian's time was that it would be foolhardy to recommit to hope in "the smallest things" at such an apocalyptically terrifying time. But Julian received visions that emboldened the words of lived lives, making them stand out not just as *not forgotten* but brought, bit by bit, into God's goodness. She received visions that underscored the holy significance of actual, daily, real people and our actual, daily hopes and fears. As the poet Denise Levertov (1997, 58) writes of Julian, "She lived in dark times, as we do: war, and the Black Death, hunger, strife, torture, massacre." Julian's visions are not timeless. They are timely. So I start with Julian's perspective on time.

TIME

On *Poynte*

And after this I saw God in an instant, that is in my understanding, and in seeing this I saw that he is in everything.

—JULIAN OF NORWICH, *Revelations of Divine Love*

In order to understand how Julian is able to receive the vision that "all shall be well," and even scoff at the Devil himself, it is helpful to think about how she views time. The word from Middle English that Julian uses in this epigraph, the word Elizabeth Spearing translates as "instant," is the word *poynte*. Spearing gives a helpful footnote on this word, explaining that it can mean "a point of space or of time" (Julian 1998, 181). Julian has a vision of God that is concentrated, seen through the aperture in the universe that is Jesus's overflowing gift of blood on the cross. Her imagery is layered. The *poynte* of seeing that allows Julian's insight is her focus on the cross as an extravagant gift that situates every space and every moment. As I will explain in chapter 2, on truth, Julian sees God's disposition toward all that was, is, and will be fully disclosed, through the cross, as a gift of love.

Here is how Julian does *not* see time: in the commonsense way many readers in the early twenty-first century in the United States see time. Most of the people in my corner of the world have a background picture in their head of time moving upward, albeit in fits and starts. Most of the people around me are "progressives" of either the right- or the left-leaning variety, expecting that things will be "better" if "we" just get with the program. That program may be funded by a conservative or a liberal think tank and be advocating for either the Democrat or the Republican on the ticket, but the basic arc of time in our minds is upward, pushed by a combination of human initiative and, for some of us, God's providence.

I do have a few rare adults in my life who do not know what day of the week it is and who generally do not think of time as progressing forward and upward toward a goal. One friend seems to let time just wash over him, or past him, or something. He just is, rather than seeing himself on a plotted line with an arrow at the end. He is peculiar. I also have a few friends who see themselves on a plotted line with an arrow at the end, pointing downward. The world is going to hell in a handbasket, whether due to climate change or the Federal Reserve or the technologizing of everything around them, sometimes combined with a plotted interpretation of the apocalyptic Book of Revelation in the New Testament. These arrow-pointing-downward people seem strange too (in a different way than my friend who lets time wash over him), in that they are suspicious of any political movement or any sort of large, social-media-fueled project to change these things for the better.

This is the normal that makes nonprogressives seem peculiar or strange today: To be a good citizen in the United States means getting your fingers typing and your phone buzzing and your feet marching to try to push the world upward for the better.

At the turn of the fourteenth to the fifteenth century in England, there were writers on both sides of the arrow perspective. There were people who saw England as possibly going to the dogs (or, more literally, to the human beings relegated to the lower classes) and people who thought the plague was God's punishment for upsetting the proper order of things. There were also people determined, against the impossible odds, to push for radical changes—political, spiritual, and what we might now call feminist. Jumping ahead to read Julian politically today requires a shift. Her writing does not really serve well what many think of as conservatism or progressivism today: the conserve-things-against-chaos project or the change-the-world-for-God's-sake project.

Julian's way of seeing time through the cross is an antitrajectory way of seeing. If you think about time as moving forward toward a goal, you are thinking in a way that has become common sense in most of the United States. But Julian's vision situates each one of us as defined through this prism, a nontemporal miracle that was a gift in time that changes time itself. This vision of hers, seeing all of us in the "instant" or *poynte* that is Jesus, is in contrast to common sense today. It was a game-change answer to anxieties about change during her time.

I want to connect Julian's view of time to a sense of order in medieval England. In part due to advances in the structure of ships, there was more mobility from Europe to England around the turn of the fourteenth to the fifteenth century, and, in a port city like Norwich, it was increasingly difficult to determine just who was who. Sumptuary laws were supposed to keep each human being dressed in a class-based costume assigned to them. The laws were to make sure that one announced oneself visually as a peasant, maid, farmer, or landowner, and as precisely which level of landowner in the English aristocratic system. Think of it as a rule against walking around in economic drag, pretending to be someone you were not officially, by birth and title, supposed to be.

With the usual mobility of a port city, however, Norwich saw travelers coming and going whose station was not immediately knowable. Residents did not know for sure how to situate these people in space and time. Some people saw changes like these as an opportunity for an overhaul of the feudal system. Others saw the same ambiguity as a sign of impending anarchy. Julian concentrates a different way of perceiving time and perceiving people in time. She concentrates the yearly cycle that is the Christian calendar year—from Advent to Lent to Ordinary Time—into a *poynte*. She receives a vision from God that time and space are like an instant. This vision has political import, but her visions do not warrant what many activists on either the right or the left in the United States would now think of as hope. For Julian hope is not an affirmation that all things shall be well, incrementally, toward a change or toward a resolution of the political order that you can point to as progress.

In his introduction to Elizabeth Spearing's translation, A. C. Spearing explains that Julian's perspective "abolishes temporal extension" (Julian 1998, xxxi). The form of her visions collapses what we usually think of as storytelling. She defines the story of God's grace in such a way that her images are more like layer upon layer of transparencies with images on them rather than a story that moves from beginning to end. Julian's understanding of providence is different from the one I have heard often used by praying Christians around me. She does not affirm that "God's wise providence," as she puts it, is the way God pulls human beings along toward resolution through a series of small or large victories. In her later reflection on providence in the Long Text she explains, "I saw God in an instant [or poynte], that is to say, in my understanding, and in seeing this I saw that he is in everything. I looked attentively, seeing and recognizing what I observed with quiet awe, and I thought, 'What is sin': For I saw truly that God does everything, no matter how small. And I saw that truly nothing happens by accident or luck, but everything by God's wise providence" (LT: 11, 58).

"God's wise providence" is not an affirmation pulled along toward resolution through a series of victories, whether minute or remarkable, private or public. From Julian's perspective, accident is eliminated because she sees time itself through that small opening, that little camera lens, which reveals everything defined and situated by the cross. Her understanding of time is not that God works through discernible episodes wherein loss (tragic or slight) brings forth blessing (profound or precious).

I do not mean to be cruel toward people who tenderheartedly offer a perspective to others or who try for solace to see the world this way themselves. In the midst of personal grief or large-scale tragedy, it can sometimes console people to look for signs that pain is being transformed incrementally into blessing. These consolations can sometimes come in the "at least" form, as in "at least" the pain was not worse or the death toll higher, or whatever "at least" consolation works. This can be combined with the silver-lining perspective, whereby one tries to find the arrow pointing upward out of pain. But this is not the way Julian has been given by God to see time. Julian pulls all that might be cast off as "accident or luck" through the central, focal point of the cross. She does not attest that there are clearly discernible arrows in our life moving up and away out of pain. Even more important, she does not tell me that my pain results, ultimately, cumulatively, in God's victory. The cross pulls all time inward toward Jesus. And the infinity of the cross redefines counting. For Julian there is no sense in measuring or seeking something that could be considered cumulative. God does not give her a vision of $1 + 1 + 1$ times a googolplex = BETTER. God wishes for us wellness, but this does not mean that, if we suffer or work hard enough, we will find concrete results of prosperity.

Another way of describing God's providence comes closer to Julian's perspective but is slightly and dangerously off-focus. This is the "we cannot know, but God knows" line. The person touting this view seems to be trying to justify something most people would say is bad but using a sham version of providence as cover for his actions. One example from a Hollywood movie, the 2007 film *Charlie Wilson's War*, is useful in a "how-not-to-think" sort of way. A CIA operative purportedly told a Texas politician, Charlie Wilson, a story about how a "Zen master" keeps saying "We'll see" about some twists and turns in the life of a boy with a horse in a village. The villagers in the story think they can name things as "good" or "bad" for this child, but the Zen master stands above it all and suggests there will be true knowledge only by maintaining an imperious "We'll see." The scene is meant to cast a haze over the machinations of the CIA in Afghanistan, and the "We'll see" suggests a "we" that will eventually see, like God, the outcomes of manipulating the present for the sake of a possible future. This "We cannot know" plus "God is on our side" version of providence is made from two-thirds up a ladder, looking down at something like a village and mere villagers—silly people who think they know how to name as good or bad that which is going on in their home.

This is not how Julian sees providence. While the CIA operative in the movie is a man, and a man with obvious, worldly power, this false way of seeing and talking in the world is not gender-specific nor reserved only for secret agents. I have heard devout churchwomen say something similar when talking together about someone else's pain. They seem truly to believe that they will end up on the right side of God's holiness ledger. "We will see" becomes an alliance with a deity who holds out wisdom and leaves the rest of us befuddled and beset by grief. Providence is not, for Julian, a ladder up which we can climb in order to see better what those little people on the ground cannot see.

Julian does not say "We will see" in this piously snooty way. She says that she has seen, in the present, a vision of all that will be. All that will be and all that has been are reckoned with God's love.

We see now, today, through the insight of an instant, the *poynte* through which everything is cast. Through this prism of thought God does not move temporally from A to B to C through time. Neither does God move a cast of characters from location 1 to 2 to 3. Julian perceives "God's wise providence" in an eye blink or, as in the most famous of her images, compressed into the form of a smooth, small nut. This question of God's real love, here and now and not some day in the land of "We will see," is not an academic puzzle for Julian. The material import of what she sees and thinks about is in her own blood and bone, as she focuses on Jesus's blood poured out for her on the cross. A. C. Spearing explains that Julian "apprehends" God's way of seeing "not as theory but as experience" (Julian 1998, xxxi). Her vision that "all shall be well" is a way of seeing that is from God's perspective, is about God's "familiar" love, and she feels it in her bones.

In this way Julian takes on a question that a theological master from the Middle Ages had dealt with in his writing. Thomas Aquinas wrote beautifully intricate questions and answers about Christian doctrine and the lived reality of faith a century before Julian. In one of his questions he asks whether God gives us grace and then frees us from sin, or frees us from sin and then gives us grace.[1] The basic question he is pondering is whether we are forgiven while still bound by sin or are freed from sin and then forgiven. After giving examples from Scripture that seem to answer the question both ways, Thomas says that, from God's perspective, we are given grace and then freed from sin. For God, Thomas writes, time does not move from point A to point B to point C, as if in stages of progress upward. Grace is not only abundant; grace is infinite in a way that topples over each human clock of timeliness. Julian takes this question from the master theologian of her time and collapses it. Sorting through what she has seen in her vision, she comes to the same conclusion as Thomas. She concentrates the time that God sees us into a *poynte* that reveals only God's love. Providence becomes a matter not of God's intent and our future safety from sin. God's intent, according to Julian's vision, is love. Period. Full stop.

What in the world does this mean? What does it mean to live in this vision of hers, that there is no "accident or luck" and also no doubt about God's loving intent?

In Denise Levertov's (1997, 51) series of poems reflecting on Julian, she writes these lines to close the first of the series of five poems about Julian's visions:

And you ask us to turn our gaze
inside out, and see
a little thing, the size of a hazelnut, and believe
it is our world? Ask us to see it lying
in God's pierced palm? That it encompasses
every awareness our minds contain? All Time?
All limitless space given form in this

---

1. If you would like to read Thomas Aquinas on this question of perspective, see his *Summa Theologiae*, the first part of the second part, question number 113.

medieval enigma?

    Yes, this is indeed
what you ask, sharing
the mystery you were shown: *all that is made:*
a little thing, the size of a hazelnut, held safe
in God's pierced palm.

In chapter 4 of her Short Text, Julian layers images in her characteristic way. The Lord shows Julian "his familiar love" as "our clothing" and as "everything that is good for us." The word *poynte* is given an image in Julian's vision as "a little thing, the size of a hazel-nut, lying in the palm of my hand" (ST: 4, 7). She goes on to explain that this "little thing" has "three attributes." This "little thing" that is "all that is made," as God tells her, is made by God, beloved by God, and cared for by God. Levertov, for her part, says the little thing is "safe" in "God's pierced palm." Levertov ties together Julian's visions of our safety in Jesus to Julian's vision of the little thing the size of a hazelnut held in Julian's own hand. Julian is able to see all that is and has been and ever will be, "safe," contained, and truly beloved by God because she has, in the vision just before this one, the "red blood" of Jesus "plentifully and vividly" given, "without any intermediary." More on the "plentifully" given blood later, but for now I want to stay right at the point of time and God.

Julian does not see the grand sweep of salvation history and determine that God must have a hand in the artistry. She does not see the arc of the universe bending upward through time and culminating in a glorious revolution that must be by God's own design. She sees a little thing, so small that she wonders if it "might suddenly disappear" (ST: 4, 7). All that is. Tiny, everlasting, beloved, and cared for by God. A hazelnut?

How can this be? The world is not simple, by any sort of adult, sober reckoning. Why did Julian not see all that is as a well-wrought mechanism? Couldn't the universe be like a miraculously antique watch that runs for all time? This would make more sense and be more reassuring to the default sensibilities I have been taught to rely on, even subconsciously, about how the world works and who rightly understands how the world works. A vision of an intricate instrument would fit better with the version of deism held by the men who wrote the Constitution of the United States. If Julian had seen a well-wrought mechanism of some sort, it would have been so much more useful for the version of hope that many people have been taught to hold. If all-that-is and all-that-we-are-a-part-of is a "tiny thing," like a nut, a tiny thing that might at any point just "disappear," what does this mean?

Next Julian sees that God became a part of all that is made by way of a creature known for her marvelous "littleness": Mary, Jesus's mother. The little thing that is all that is made is made part of God's life through Jesus, who is brought into the world through a young woman named Mary. It is a work of poetic mischief that Julian calls Mary both "great" and marked for greatness by her "littleness." "Lady Saint Mary," Julian writes, is all wrapped up in the "nothingness" that makes our lives about grace. "This is why those who choose to occupy themselves with earthly business and are always pursuing worldly success have nothing here of God in their hearts and souls" (ST: 4, 8). Julian could not have seen the world and all that is as a Rolex watch. It had to be a nut or a pebble, held, as Levertov puts it, in "God's pierced palm."

Seeing this series of visions with Julian means knowing both the insignificance and the recalibrated, *infinite* significance of you and of me and of our mundane, earthly world. To "occupy" ourselves with business and success—to see our occupation as within the matter of financial exchange and logistical upticks in success—is to "have nothing here of God" in our hearts. Her language matters. To *occupy* is to seize. To have ourselves overtaken or seized with business and success is to have our soul hijacked by accounting. Julian repeats in this vision the word *nought* or *nothing*. She is not saying that the world is meaningless. She sees a vision that all that could be could also *not* be: it could "disappear" if not for being held. All that is *is* held, though, and held in a way that scrambles calculation and the usual ways we weigh, measure, and sort ourselves, strangers, our children, our churches, or our neighborhoods.

Watson and Jenkins have a helpful note on this section in their edition of Julian's writings. When Julian writes, "This is why those who choose to occupy themselves with earthly business and are always pursuing worldly success have nothing here of God in their hearts and souls" (ST: 4, 8), she uses language that "is suggestive of the 'besines' [business] of Norwich, whose trade connections extended throughout Europe and from one of whose families Julian may have come" (Watson and Jenkins 2006, 70). To live by a trade-based reckoning of worth may mean I can be armored for the present and for the sake of my future safety. It might be a logically prudent way of seeing the world and my life in this world. But Julian sees frankly that to be so occupied—to think in commercialized terms—is to lose one's perspective on love. She puts the stakes starkly: to think about oneself and the world around her in this way is to "have nothing here of God."

Julian's visions contrast with much that counts as common sense today, and they were apparently no less confusing for earlier readers. Watson and Jenkins explain that one seventeenth-century edition of A Revelation (the Long Text) combines two convenient misreadings of Julian's writing. The misreadings were perhaps serviceable to the seventeenth century, reinforcing a sense of properly ladylike passivity. Presenting her apolitically, as a representative of a form of sequestered piety, also cordons off her visions from the deep, political implications of an antimercantilist and nonhierarchical form of Christianity. This 1670 edition was produced by Serenus Cressy, "royal chaplain at the court of Charles II," and, as Watson and Jenkins (2006, 17) relate, "describes Julian's by now defunct profession of an anchorite, portraying it nostalgically as a life of complete separation from the world." Royal Chaplain Serenus Cressy also tells his seventeenth-century readers that Julian has seen a vision of the "Nothingness of Creatures." But the "Nothingness of Creatures" is not at all what she saw and not at all what she wrote. In Julian's writing, "sin is nothingness." This makes us a different sort of somethingness that defies measure. No matter how useful it might have been for Royal Chaplain Serenus Cressy if Julian had written that creatures are nothing, she did not (17).

History is told as a story, and the way history is told says something about the people telling the story about the way things were. This bit of historiography about a royal chaplain from the seventeenth century is helpful to think about how not to read Julian's warning against preoccupation. We have hints today about how active Julian might have been during her time as an anchorite, through a translation of a thirteenth-century guide for women serving as anchorites, called The Ancrene Riwle (1990, 182–92). The writer specifies many different details about what appear to be frequent interactions with people wandering by the church and seeking out an anchorite. One reason the writer dissuades his advisees from keeping a cow (!) in her anchorhold is that the cow might misbehave and lead to "complaints in a village." The advisor who wrote The Ancrene Riwle also wants to make clear that an anchorite needs to veer toward more meditation, warning her not to "turn into a school-mistress" (188). The specificity suggests some anchorites were quite occupied with the matters of their church, village, or city. Where there is so much advice about ridding the anchor-hold of smoke, so to speak, there were likely some fires.

To read Julian's words today about being occupied as a warning against being engaged in a life of materially caring for one another is to make her into a different sort of theologian than she was. It may be serviceable to some readers to render Julian a recluse who recommended that Christians care nothing for mere creatures, but it is true neither of her life nor of her writing. This is another version, perhaps, of the downtown priest's dismissal of Julian as having suffered a mental breakdown that led to her being sequestered. Put her visions into a box so that her words are pious but impractical, and we may then safely read her without too much tumult. But Julian's visions suggest that the hardest and best blessed work is right where she says it is: in seeing and loving this world—our world—in a noncalculated, radically familial way.

Julian's answer to the quandary of time is different from Piper's neo-Calvinist insistence on our human "insignificance" in the face of God's sovereignty. Her providence may be compatible with one version of Calvinism, but not the one Piper describes in that succinct lecture about what people need in times of anxiety. There is scriptural warrant for avoiding declarations that sweep everyone into a bin of insignificance. "Lady Saint Mary," as Julian calls Jesus's mother, does not meekly proclaim a word about her own *insignificance* at the announcement that she will be the mother of the savior of the world. Mary did not say, "Oh! Okay! So now I know how insignificant we all are in God's grand scheme of things! Hooray for our humiliation!" Mary praises God's magnificence and, in her song, the *Magnificat* (Luke 1:46–50), foretells God's upside-down turning of people.

This upside-down turning will be such that Lady Saint Mary's own "littleness," as Julian terms it, is made "blessed." The "mighty" must prepare to step down off their thrones and out of their palaces, to sit at a picnic table with the people they formerly ruled. The lowly can anticipate a world in which domination is over, *kaput*, and they know the blue-blooded as their neighbor at that picnic table. Or, if this image makes more sense to you, imagine an overseas British Airways flight from New York to London, with all the gradations of seats, from fancy to sort of comfortable to truly squished seats back at the very back. Now imagine the head flight attendant announcing that the crowded family with a crying baby and a toddler will go into the front cabin where there are soft blankets and seats that turn into beds. And the businesswoman in first class who is reading a book on how to get ahead in a man's world will come sit with the crew and eat biscuits. And the people who have paid for tip-top class will go toward the back and hold other people's babies with earaches and comfort other people's grandmothers who are queasy from motion sickness. The way of seeing time with Julian is a way that brings all that is and was and will be into a *poynte* that changes our perspective about the whimsicality of the miracle that is our existence.

Two stories from my own effort at mothering in mundane life have helped me think, in my own space, about time on a *poynte* created by God in Jesus. It was one Christmas Eve eve, as we call December 23

in my family. My younger daughter was about four years old, and we were reading a book from Grandma's collection, about a puppy eager for Santa Claus to come down the chimney. She asked me if I believed Santa was coming in two days. I corrected her in my pedantic, theologian-mommy way that I believed Jesus was coming in two days.

"But, Mommy, Jesus died. We learned that in Sunday school."

Yes, I said. Jesus died. And Jesus was resurrected from the dead.

"That's Easter!" she remembered.

Yep.

"Was Jesus a baby when he was killed?"

No, I said. Jesus was a grown-up when he was killed.

"But Jesus is coming in two days, as a baby?" she asked.

"Yes," I said.

"Mom," she sighed, exasperated, "I cannot think all of those things at the same time."

I also cannot think all of those things at the same time. This is one way to understand why many Christians practice a church year where we think these things together and sing about them and live into them, one church season to the next. Advent, Epiphany, Ordinary Time, Lent, Easter, Pentecost, Ordinary Time, and back around again. In this repetitive cycle of what we call "liturgy," I practice a way of living time that is cyclical, not progressive. I come back together with the other people in my church, and with people in churches across the world, to be shaped by Jesus's birth (Advent), his life and complicated teachings (Ordinary Time), his death (Lent), his resurrection (Easter), the birth of the people who were the early church who proclaimed the resurrection (Pentecost), and back around to learn from his life and teachings (Ordinary Time). To return to the image of a dancer focusing on a focal point to stay upright, Christians dance around a *poynte* in time that centers all that is. Julian sees this in the cross. All points in the liturgical year intersect at the place and time that is the cross. I will try to explain how this is so and what difference it makes for our bodies, for the social body that was Norwich, and for the place that is your own patch of earth and your own crowd of kin.

The second story may serve as a bookmark until the third and fourth chapters of this book, on blood and on bodies. Our family was dealing with the decomposition of my marriage. My younger daughter was just recently past the stage of life that is potty training. Intent not to make her ashamed and scared of her own body, I had been clear that accidents were a normal part of the whole process. Right around the same time, our beloved old dog was losing his last hold on continence. We would return home regularly to a mess that was also, for me, a recurring and depressing sign of his mortality. You could tell me all day long that he had led a long, happy life, but, weird as this may sound to people who do not have pets, this old mutt was my first baby. I was grieving the dog hospice process along with cleaning up the increasingly reliable signs of his demise.

My youngest had been taking all of this in, apparently. One day in the car she asked me if Ernie was going to heaven. I decided not to go into the whole rigmarole about how Ernie would be in an inexplicable waiting zone for the return of Jesus. I went with the collapse of all time into one moment, or instant. Yes, I told her, Ernie will soon be going to heaven. She did not miss a beat.

"Will there be squirrels in heaven?"

Hmmmm. Lions, lambs, asps—all in heaven, apparently, according to Scripture. And then there is the whole Noah's ark thing, where God saves two of every single creature. So, yes, squirrels too.

She thought for a few minutes. "Will there be eating in heaven?"

I now saw where she was going. Ernie loved to chase squirrels. He had never caught one. If Ernie perceived heaven, it would certainly look like catching squirrels. This was a totally sensible question, of course, but a bit trickier for me to sort out how to answer. Jesus did eat fish with his friends after the resurrection, so, yes, I said. There will be eating in heaven. (This, while driving in traffic, where many of my hardest mothering conversations seem to happen.)

"Well, Mom," she decided, "there will be poop in heaven."

In my world at that time, mortality and heaven and the redemption of dog poop was important. Ernie's accidents, Ernie's mortality, and dealing with what seemed like irredeemable suffering were all mixed up in ways I wanted to know would eventually be redeemed—made good—in heaven. My daughter seemed to be asking me, in her own way, whether our home, our bodies, and the parts of our lives that seemed impossibly difficult would eventually be redeemed. Her questions about God and our bodies registered in my own brain, colliding with my questions about what was going to happen to my marriage. I have used this story in teaching Julian of Norwich ever since my daughter asked these questions. Do I trust that God wants joy for us? Do I trust that God is all-loving and will do everything? Do I trust this enough to shape my imagination to risk courage and laughter? Do I trust God's love enough to risk the mocking derision, even condemnation, of others? In her own time Julian risked all of this and more to write down her visions. She risked speaking in her own voice about God's omniamity.

To connect a time of plague and hunger, peasant uprisings and schisms to dog crap, abuse in my home, and the ramifications of a publicly broken marriage may seem sentimental. Regardless of whether or not you think I am being trite, hear me on this. The particular material crises of Julian's time mattered for how people saw the significance or insignificance of their own matter. I have found that her words from within these crises resonate with people going through their own particular misery and during a time of economic and social upheaval that have left neighbors and loved ones uncertain, despondent, anxious, or confounded. Julian saw all that is and was and will be as held by God, and this matters for our bodies and our hope that every aspect of our lives will be redeemed.

In the introduction to their book on medieval English culture, David Aers and Lynn Staley (1996, 3) explain the historical period of Julian's writing:

Through [the symbols of Christian sanctity] people sought to understand and shape the massive dislocations, shifts, possibilities, and conflicts in the half-century following the great plague. These complex shifts, together with the different opportunities, conflicts, and anxieties they entailed, had implications for the relations between women and men, in all dimensions, those around divisions of work, those around the divisions of sexuality, and those around the construing of gendered identities. This time included the great schism in the church, including sharpened struggles between agriculturalists of all kinds and the taxing, law-forming, rent-extracting classes, including struggles between magnates and crown. . . . In fact people in these years were living through, making, and resisting major disruptions in the political orders and in the credibility of received legitimations of authority.

Julian was writing during a time of both "dislocation" and "shifts." This could lead to "possibility" but also to "conflict." Aers and Staley say that this period was in a post-horror state, "following the great plague." The plague had left people, well, left. People remaining alive after the plague likely wondered why they were left alive to grieve. I say "likely" because the written documents from this time reflect questions torn from Scripture, as God's people tried to reckon with unspeakable tragedy during slavery and plagues and massive displacement from the places they had been taught tied them to holiness. Spaces of memory and sanctity for God's people had been destroyed by invading armies, over and over and over again, and Scripture is replete with explanation, lament, rage, faith, and despair about where God was in the history they were enduring.

When Julian was about eight years old, God was officially present in loss if a priest arrived to administer the last rites before someone died. When Julian was about eight years old, a plague killed so many people that there are not ways for historians reliably to count the dead, and priests died while trying to run away from the plague or trying to be faithful to the mandate of their calling to administer the Lord's Supper as people were dying from the plague. At the time Julian was seeing her visions, there were also famines sweeping through England, in such a way that even the cattle of royalty died without being counted.

And the cattle of royalty mattered more than the peasants who fed the cattle. After reading as many books as I can put my hands on I am certain that people loved one another no less then than people love one another now. People in the horror of death may become numb, but people often also seek meaning and a way to keep their faith. Julian saw all that is in this horror, transformed, beloved, beheld.

As Aers and Staley write, "People in these years were living through, making, and resisting major disruptions in the political orders and in the credibility of received legitimations of authority." Julian lived at a time when the authority of those who deemed themselves the arbiters of truth and order had been shaken by natural disaster. They had been exposed as lacking in legitimate authority as somehow divinely ordered to keep order. Julian saw visions of God that made the aristocracy beholden, if they troubled to read her. It is perhaps a gift of history that the ladies and lords did not read her closely enough to have her counted among the dangerous. She lived long enough to write a Long Text of her visions. She also situated herself in a church to hear and advise people who could be charged with heresy and imprisoned for maintaining the disruption of domination. Her vision of providence does not deny the horrors around her and the fissures that could break open into mass murder or freedom. It also does not allow for there to be irredeemable "accidents." The "symbols of Christian sanctity" that Aers and Staley have in mind during Julian's period are a set of ways that people negotiated the changes and possibilities around them. Julian received the body and blood of sanctity, in Jesus, and saw all that was around her as a recalibration of kinship itself.

A contemporary example will help bring together the dog poop story and Julian's time. Once a form of social Darwinism became normal in Western thinking, it became hard for some Christians not to think of either prosaic human suffering or epically horrific suffering as a culling of the population for the sake of a stronger species. Darwin may be read in many different ways, but the way that social Darwinism has trickled into mainstream thought in the United States means that just about every bad thing that happens from a distance can be assessed as part of the slow but steady upward evolution of humanity. Just as Freud hardly meant that everything long was phallic or that every relationship was about my mother's breast, Darwin did not write that a struggle for survival necessarily creates an arc upward toward human excellence. But that is the way his thought is often, now almost subconsciously, applied by those of us who think of ourselves as properly educated. I once heard a table full of smart, non-Christian adults speculate that a tsunami, which had wiped out thousands of people, was nature's way of clearing space for evolutionary progress. I heard another group of smart, Christian men speculate that God would use the same disaster to bring Jesus to pagans, as Christian (Western) entrepreneurs entered the vacuum to build factories run with "Christian values."

Accidents are the dross of history, according to this default social Darwinian mode of thinking, and if providence is also a part of the story, then accidents are how God moves history forward. Julian asks us to see with her differently. She reveals her revelations to allow for a way of seeing time in a *poynte*, as God's loving hold on all that is. All that is could disappear in an instant. But it does not. And nothing is lost. Our poop is redeemed, not through an upward arc of progress but through the blood of Jesus Christ.

People in the United States who did not grow up going to church might nevertheless know the phrase "sinners in the hands of an angry God" from their American history class. Jonathan Edwards gave this sermon twice, both times in New England around the mid-eighteenth century. Edwards wrote all sorts of things about God's love, but in this well-known phrase he emphasized the urgency of deciding to be a Christian. If not for God's mercy in Jesus Christ, we would all be flung into the pit of hell. Four hundred years earlier than Edwards, Julian wrote this:

For this is what was shown: that our life is all grounded and rooted in love, and without love we cannot live; and therefore to the soul which through God's special grace sees so much of his great and marvelous goodness, and sees that we are joined to him in love for ever, it is the greatest impossibility conceivable that God should be angry, for anger and friendship are two contraries. It must needs be that he who wears away and extinguishes our anger and makes us gentle and kind, which is the contrary of anger; for I saw quite clearly where our Lord appears, everything is peaceful and there is no place for anger; for I saw no kind of anger in God, neither for a short time nor for a long one; indeed, it seems to me that if God could be even slightly angry we could never have any life or place or being. (LT: 49, 112)

One way of sustaining faith in a classical conception of God during the crises that marked Julian's early life was to view them as God's punishment. No doubt many people in England decided the world was horribly random and cruel, period. They either did not have access to pen and parchment or were smart enough to keep their mouths and minds shut, because true atheism was, of course, punishable heresy. If you wanted to be mentally safe from state reprisal, or if you desired still to hold fast to Christian faith, the most reasonable explanation, and one with some scriptural warrant, was that God was, in a sense, culling the herd. The people who had perished were a macabre object lesson from God to remind everyone to be scared and grateful, so that the survivors would come closer to God, or at least become more obedient.

Julian receives a vision of God's abundant blood given in a way that a remarkably adoring mother gives a child her favorite and best food. We are children in the hands of a loving God. Just to be clear, Julian makes a logical argument in addition to describing a vision of God's omniamity. She does not pose this as a form of debate, but there is an underlying challenge for her possible interlocutors. If you read between the lines in the long quote above, she basically says, *So, dear survivors of the many disasters besetting our century, do you really think that you* are around because you are better and more beloved by God than those beloveds who are no longer with us? No. I didn't think so. If God could be angry, none of us would be here. So, given we have "life" and "place" and "being," God's providence must be enfolded with God's love. The tragic and terrorizing accidents of this world are redeemed and held in the *poynte* that is God's time.

I have received two stories while teaching Julian that have helped me to connect her understanding of time "in an instant" with her description of truth, blood, and bodies. I have permission to share them, and they may help readers segue into my next three chapters, which are full of visions and questions about truthfulness, the Lord's Supper, and our bodies.

One student explained in class that his church had gone through a difficult process of discernment about using a common cup for Communion. When a congregation uses a common cup, everyone either sips from the cup during the Eucharist or dips their bread into the cup one by one (a practice known as intinction). The elders in his congregation had become aware that a member of his congregation was HIV-positive. This student's congregation had been using a common cup, but the elders needed to determine whether they should continue. They determined, after much prayer, that the proper way to proceed was to continue with a common cup but to privately invite the member who was HIV-positive to partake each week toward the front of the Communion line. As this student told this story to our class, his classmates looked not only confused but worried. I think I probably looked baffled. He gently explained to the rest of us that the elders rightly discerned that the member who was HIV-positive was the most vulnerable. Because this member's immune system was compromised, this member had the most to lose if exposed to the germs of other people. I watched as other members of my class registered that this student's church was extraordinarily different from their own churches. It is one thing to believe that the cup of blessing holds Jesus's blood. To decide such a decision with a mixture of hope and practical wisdom—stripped of notions of shame and fault that stick like glue to a condition like HIV—this is a way of seeing one another that takes a miracle.

I was teaching Julian to a group of pastors one year when a prison chaplain told a story. He had been a chaplain since his now-adult children were small. After hearing about Julian, he said he felt a burden of guilt lifted. He told the class that he had always felt guilty that he was bringing home to his children the problems in the prison where he worked. I remember trying to repeat to him some of those problems, thinking I had understood what he was talking about. But then he corrected me. No, he did not mean the emotional pain of all that the prisoners were dealing with in their spiritual lives. He meant the literal, concrete problems you can carry out of a prison with you. Because a prison involves inhumanely close quarters, a prison also involves many opportunities for cross-contamination of parasites. No matter how much people living in prison wish to keep themselves individually safe and set apart from one another's illnesses, the whole structure is set up for barely minimal efficiency, not health (more like a factory farm than like a hotel). He had brought viruses and lice and other tangibly gross things back home with him, and his family had come to be an extension of his work in that materially disgusting way. His children, he explained, had dealt with more than their share of lice because he worked at a prison. Hearing about Julian's vision of safety in the instant that is the cross, and that this instant is the truth by which we judge prudence and love—this news was an unexpected gift for him.

When Julian asked to receive the wounds of Jesus, she refused to separate herself as a righteous survivor. She entered into a *poynte* that is the cross, where the prudent strategies of protecting oneself are not the most important questions for a Christian to ask. People have attributed a pithy phrase to southern novelist Flannery O'Connor: "You shall know the truth and the truth shall make you odd." I now turn to what Julian means by "truth."

TRUTH

Divine Delight

> Jesus wishes us to consider the delight which the Holy
> Trinity feels in our salvation and wishes us to long for as
> much spiritual pleasure, through his grace, as has already
> been described. . . . The whole Trinity took part in the
> Passion of Christ.
>
> —JULIAN OF NORWICH, *Revelations of Divine Love*

Why did God become human? What does this mean, that God became
human? What does it mean that human beings are "saved" by Jesus?
Is this a quirk? A trick? A puzzle that only theologians with formal
training can solve and explain? I will now ask readers to make a giant
linguistic leap from theology-speak to beauty salon–speak or to car
mechanic–speak. The leap will help me explain why it matters that
Julian writes in English and argues, as one student put it to me, "like
a girl."

Mariya Tivnan is a friend of mine who helped me see how Christian
theology often works. Mariya grew up under Soviet rule, in an Eastern
European border country. She has been trying to help me manage my
hair for a decade. Mariya listens to me complain about my work, and
I listen to her complain about her work. Once I was explaining why it

ticks me off that some theologians use words that no one else understands to try to make themselves feel superior and seem smart to the people around them. This seems particularly wrong because Scripture is made up of commonplace words and everyday stories that people shared, often by memory, to help other people know who God is. Evidently fancy salons do the same thing that snooty theologians do. Mariya explained that people who want to make sure that no one can blow-dry their own hair well make styling look like magic. They twirl various instruments around with a flourish and never explain what is happening. She has helped me learn all the basics with a cheap brush and blow-dryer because I have two daughters and a single-parent budget.

The same friend of mine who does not always keep track of which day of the week it is will fix your car in any place and at any time. His one requirement is that you pay attention to what he is teaching you. He does not want to fix your car if you see your car as magic. He wants to fix your car and teach you how, next year, you can fix it yourself. He thinks it is not smart for women or men to drive around in things that can kill people while not knowing how to begin to tell when that large, catapulting piece of metal might malfunction.

This is one way to explain the term *vernacular theology*. The medievalist Bernard McGinn first used this term, and Nicholas Watson repeated it in his writing. Vernacular theology describes Christian writings by people without explicit churchly power, written in the language that people working in fields would speak, if not read. My conversations about the beauty shop and automobiles helped me to name what is at stake when scholars say Julian is writing vernacular theology. Julian wrote for real people, in the language that farmers and peasants and shopkeepers and nurses spoke.

The period in which Julian is receiving her visions from God and writing down her descriptions for others, in English, culminated in a document from the archbishop of Canterbury known as the "Arundel Constitutions." Watson (1995, 837) suggests this 1409 document was a response to a development in Christianity in England that had been growing for generations. This was the period during which Julian was seeing, praying, and writing. By 1409 there were restrictions on what could be taught and by whom. The matter of who could translate any part of Scripture into English, or have any part of Scripture translated into English in their home, was to be carefully regulated. As Watson explains, while earlier documents had delineated the "*minimum* necessary for the laity to know if they are to be saved," the Constitutions focused on "the *maximum* they may hear, read, or even discuss" (828, italics in the original). Watson continues, "No longer was it the ignorance of the laity and their priests that was a matter for concern; it was the laity's too eager pursuit of knowledge" (828). Watson offers a helpful summary of the official reasons for restricting translation of Scripture and theological texts into English, drawn from documents in an ongoing series of debates at Oxford University, held before the official decree banning vernacular theology: "Translation into the mother tongue will allow any old woman (*vetula*) to usurp the office of teacher, which is forbidden to them (since all heresies, according to Jerome, come from women); it will bring about a world in which the laity prefers to teach than to learn, in which women (*mulierculae*) talk philosophy and dare to instruct men—in which a country bumpkin (*rusticus*) will presume to teach" (843).

I mentioned before the regulations that were enacted to make sure people dressed according to their particular rung on the ladder of England at that time; these were called "sumptuary laws." Language was another form of regulation. Many church people in the United States today swoon for English spoken with an English accent, but during Julian's time English was the common language, the language of commoners. The people associated with the church who talked about God in English were relegated to the local setting by their superiors. Local priests taught about God in English because local people had to know the bare basics of set doctrine. But if you wanted truly to consider the glorious intricacies of Scripture and doctrine, you spoke and wrote in Latin. If you wanted to "speculate," you had to speculate in Latin. And due to the various machinations of royalty crisscrossing France and England, the language of the court was French. The people who made the rules—both church and state—knew English but did not "wear it." People who were to follow the rules made by the rulers were not to try to put on the language of their betters. Christianity was too important to be left to the vernacular and to the people actually wearing it, so to speak.

But Julian was one of several writers we know about during the fourteenth century who planted patches of vernacular theology in the cracks of what was possible. She received a vision that flourished in a gap most people thought closed at the time. In her extended vision, known by Julian lovers and scholars as "The Servant and the Lord," she received a different word about the Holy Trinity and the atonement. She wrote about why God became human and how we are saved by Jesus. These matters had been basically settled. If they were considered still puzzling or open to consideration, that consideration was to occur at Oxford or Cambridge and in Latin, not English. Again, shortly after Julian wrote her Long Text, to think about puzzles in theology in the vernacular was forbidden.

Julian detects divine favor when divine discontent, or anger, seems a more direct explanation of human misery. She finds God's profligate kindness (what she calls God's "kinning") by pulling all questions through the needle's eye of the cross. The crucified Jesus points her to the Trinity—God the Father, God the Son, and God the Holy Spirit—and the Trinity is revealed in the copious blood of Jesus on the cross. Her reading of God's joy is complete, taking in not only the Second Person of the Trinity (Jesus) but the First and Third Persons of a Triune God as well. God the Father and God the Holy Spirit are one in their joy, through the cross. The crucifix that Julian fixates on, and through which she pulls all of her questions about who God is and who we are in relation to God, is the embodiment of God, Spirit, and Son.

Early in her Short Text, in the second short chapter, Julian explains that, while in the bed that she thought was going to be her last earthly home, she saw the crucifix that her pastor put before her face become lit by "an ordinary, household light" (ST: 2, 6). This early description of what happened to and in her is characteristic of her writing. Julian is worn out from being so sick for so long, and she thinks that she might as well just look at the crucifix rather than trying to look up to heaven because looking straight ahead at the cross takes less energy. And in looking at the cross she sees everything around her grow dark except the cross. It is lit not with some spectacular, angelic light parade but with "an ordinary, household light." This "ordinary" cross is the *poynte* where grace and love are found and where Julian seeks solidarity with Jesus and all of God's "kin." Julian experiences God's truth "without any intermediary" as "familiar" and "courteous."

The word that comes close to connoting the layers of "homely" words that Julian uses in this section is *cozy*. This vision of love shapes her sense of sin and of safety. It may sound bizarre to some readers to call God cozy, but Julian truly saw God as both familiar and awe-inspiring. God's proximity, God's familiarity would seem to some of Julian's contemporaries to be so baffling as to be heretical.[1] But she takes it all in and sorts it out, assuming within herself, in trust, that which God had shown her was true. She thought past the "stop" of God's omniamity, seeing the world as within God's love and God's joy.

In the centuries before Julian wrote, many of the usual images of Jesus saving humanity depicted a victorious conquering of Satan. Jesus was depicted not as suffering for humanity but as kicking ass for humanity. A different version of salvation became somewhat standard in the century or so before Julian received her visions. The simplified version went like this: Sin has ripped apart the order of the universe, and Jesus pays the price for all of humanity. This has come to be known by theologians who label concepts in theology as the Satisfaction Theory of Atonement. Jesus satisfies God's justice, and humans are again at-one (atoned) with God. The logic of this theory is that order is restored. In this way of thinking, which runs through Christianity at least since the fall of the Roman Empire, the most besetting ramification of the fall is disorder. Anarchy is the dragon waiting in the deeps.

Julian received visions of a different at-one-ment, or atonement,

---

1. In order better to understand Julian's use of the cross, in particular in relation to rituals of death during this period, please see Appleford (2008).

with God. In her visions Jesus does not kick ass for humanity, conquering sin like St. George conquers the dragon. But neither does Jesus stand between a God intent on justice and humans who are due punishment. Jesus draws us to God so familiarly that we are, as she puts it, "safe and sound" (ST: 10, 17). "Here I saw a great union between Christ and us; for when he was in pain, we were in pain. And all creatures who were capable of suffering, suffered with him. And as for those who did not know him, their suffering was that all creation, sun and moon, withdrew their service, and so they were all left in sorrow during that time. And thus those that loved him suffered for love, and those that did not love him suffered from a failure of comfort from the whole of creation" (10, 17). She continues, "I would rather have suffered until Judgement Day than have come to heaven otherwise than by him" (10, 17). Looking intently, focusing on the cross, Julian sees all who know Jesus and all who do not know Jesus there in the suffering of Jesus. The "sorrow" of "the whole of creation" brings those who did not know or who do not now know Jesus into the cross. This "great union between Christ and us" is an affirmation that kept Julian thinking and writing for over a decade.

With prayerful stitching over many years, Julian worked on sin in relation to this safety. This brought her clarity about the most confusing vision she received, that of the Servant and the Lord. This is a vision that she writes about only in the Long Text, perhaps because she received this vision while discerning the truths of her original visions. Or perhaps she did not write about this vision in her early text because she was so confused by it that she needed a decade to try to understand and write it down for others. Regardless, by the time of her Long Text she is definite that she knows God through Jesus, and she comes to recognize all of humanity by way of this Jesus-defined God. What follows is just part of a lengthy section from her Long Text that is a kind of parable of a Lord and a Servant, a parable that is part of Julian's visions and a crystallization of her perspective on atonement:

> In the servant is comprehended the second person of the Trinity, and in the servant is comprehended Adam, that is to say, all men.

And therefore when I say "the Son," it means the Godhead, which is equal with the Father, and when I say "the servant," it means Christ's Humanity, which is truly Adam. The servant's nearness represents the Son, and his standing on the left side represents Adam. The lord is the Father, God; the servant is the Son, Christ Jesus. The Holy Ghost is the equal love which is in both of them. When Adam fell, God's son fell; because of the true union made in heaven, God's son could not leave Adam, for by Adam I understand all men. Adam fell from life to death into the valley of this wretched world, and after that into hell. God's son fell with Adam into the valley of the Virgin's womb (and she was the fairest daughter of Adam), in order to free Adam from guilt in heaven and in earth; and with his great power he fetched him out of hell. (LT: 51, 121)

Julian links the "great power" of Jesus with the homely, familiar, "fairest" beauty of the Virgin's womb. Christ the victor falls into a womb rather than donning a knight's armor. And Jesus the liberator wears the clothing of a servant. One way of thinking about this vision is that God transgresses the sumptuary laws at their most basic level. God the divine becomes human, fooling everyone who cannot imagine God's love. In fact in her vision God is a servant, so one-d or kinned with Adam, with humanity, that there is no distance between Jesus and Adam. Julian sees the servant in the parable of her vision as comprehensively two distinct characters: the Second Person of the Trinity and Adam. She further sorts out that God knows all of humanity by way of uniting Adam and Jesus, the Son. In the decades between writing her Short Text and her Long Text, Julian found that God perceives humanity through this unity of Jesus and Adam, without remainder. There is no aspect of residual anger in God's perception of humanity, fetched out of hell.

In his introduction to his translation of Julian's texts, A. C. Spearing reads her parable as allowing Julian to "see reality as God sees it": "The orthodox solution to the problem of predestination and free will was that for God, who exists in eternity, past and future coexist in an eternal present to which the 'present of this brief and fleeting moment' is the nearest human equivalent. In the parable Julian apprehends this divine vision of reality not as theory but as experience" (Julian 1998, xxxi). The vision closely entangles Jesus with Adam so that they can no longer be seen apart from one another. She further identifies God through the falling-into-the-womb that accomplishes atonement. The parable narrates, as if in time, a truth that Julian perceives by compressing time, first through her intense concentration on the cross and then through her determined, patient, resilient, and brave sorting out of what she had seen in the parable.

This aspect of Julian's vision is a scandal. From one perspective she has made God so cozy, or so familiar, that God becomes powerless or unjust, like a parent who loves her children so much that she cannot bring herself to discipline them while they injure one another. Some readers have found offense in a slightly different angle: they read her as violating the basic conception of human justice. By that reading humans are left with no recourse to name and resist oppression. Seen from this angle, the parable reflects Julian's inability to reckon with human responsibility for the horror humans inflict on one another.

If I read him correctly, this is how David Aers (2009) judges Julian in his book *Salvation and Sin*. He writes that, by collapsing "the will to sin, the choices against divine grace are assimilated into the language of 'payne,' of suffering, for which there is no 'blame.'" Aers is concerned "that the strategy here systematically diminishes human responsibility for evil and, equally systematically, banishes the discourse of divine justice as though this might be in conflict with divine love" (161). He sees her visions as incapable of rectifying the misery human beings inflict on one another in an ongoing struggle for power: "Julian's theology does not, probably cannot, address collective life and its domination by will and power alienated from God and the covenants. It cannot address the stuff of the earthly city" (170). Her visions are anemic. Given that the sins of "collective life" are often driven by what Aers terms "domination," she seems to have drained all the blood out of the atonement.

This is the criticism of Julian that I find most compelling. Remember that when I first heard the phrase "All shall be well" I was pretty sure that Julian was a ninny. When I first heard a thumbnail description of her visions, I wanted no part in carrying such a silly book into a classroom full of future pastors. The last thing I wanted to do was encourage Christians tilted already toward cheap and apolitical grace to read a woman who would tell them they were right to stay obeisant to bullies.

What I have found as I have read her and taught her again and again and again is that Julian does not ignore domination and oppression and the horrors we inflict on one another. She addresses the sins of collective life that gather like poisonous fungi on the underside of domination. Her visions do not deny justice. Her visions redirect us away from a cycle of reinforced order that depends on divine anger and a threat of retribution.

When we are scared that we or our children are going to be beheaded or relegated to starvation, when we are reminded in hidden or obvious ways that we are—in the reckoning of those leaders responsible for calculating the worth of people "beneath" them—truly no more important than our mercantilist use-value, then our response may be to scramble for survival in the worst possible ways. When we realize that, to the people who seem to be in charge of how things work, we are less important than squirrels on a highway, we do not necessarily react by banding together to fight the powers that be. In history, as I have read it, people who suffer under the boot of other human beings who have been taught to consider themselves above the fray are as likely to commit perpetual and creative cruelties against one another as they are to band together in solidarity against the boot on top of them.

This is a thing that some people have called horizontal violence: people subject to the powers that have everything to gain by keeping things tragically unequal can turn on one another and on their own souls, hating themselves and one another because that is easier, psychically, than feeling the profound sense of non-sense that is perpetually reinforced injustice. During times of natural disaster or social instability, the pressure to cohere and conform can tighten, and people can be drawn to the worst sort of self-harm and malice even toward those they are supposed to love most. Julian answers this.

Before I go on, I want to note that some readers have grown up in Christian places that view suffering as a school for holiness. The idea that suffering usually brings people closer to God or to one another is hardly an existential fact, but the idea perdures in both Christian kitsch and rehearsed sermons. Alternatively some readers may have grown up in politically radical communities that see all breaks in the cosmic dome of patriarchy and monarchy and oligarchy as signs that things are about to start to be better. The idea that architectonic shifts in society bring fruitful liberation is lovely, but hardly proven. As far as I can tell from my vantage point of almost fifty years on this earth, it is as likely that suffering divides people within themselves and from one another and that times of possible change can also tend people toward fear and a retrenchment in old divisions.

Julian's visions penetrate into the crux of this truth, inviting people, in spite of all the risks, to see one another as kin, in the foolish safety of God's present. Her visions address domination from the vantage of someone who has been underneath the structures that divide people from each other and from within the hope that change is coming. She attests to this even though, lo and behold, the same damn divisive lies lurk right around the corner, coming back around for us to deal with yet again, and again.

During the fourteenth century one moral-theological task was to give an account of senseless loss after a crisis of plague and the failure of last rites. Answers from the topside involved God's wrath and God's reinforced order, but Julian sees a truth that creates a game change. She radically digs into the roots of dread over the state of one's own soul and safety and the safety of all those who have died unshriven.

It is also common in Western history for those at the top of a hierarchy to exploit times of disaster by tightening restrictions that reinforce their status. If the Great Plague was God's response to human sin, then God could be used again as the divine justification for keeping everyone in their place—dominated and submissive. But as Watson (1995) argues, during the fourteenth century there was, for a time, an opening up of categories. People without formal training as scholars were writing about and thinking on and seeing God and the world around them in creative ways, ways that eventually brought about a crackdown on laypeople and clergy alike. I read Julian as giving a scene-shifting answer to crises of her time. She compresses categories for a reason. The fact that her writings are in her vernacular means that both the content and the form of her writing contribute to an implausible kinning that, while squelched for a time, soon comes back around to sweep across Western Christianity.

I have two smaller-scale stories from teaching Julian that may help at this point for those who do not think in macropolitical terms. That first year when I taught Julian at Duke, in 1999, my older daughter was three. She had just been through a giant shift in our move from New Haven to Durham. Things were already hard in my marriage. So the transition had been bad, with the basic logistics of moving and with the patience required of people when things shift. The setting at work was, for me, intense, and I had never been quite so insecure. One day when I was juggling mommy work and academic work, my daughter told me that she needed to go to the bathroom. I was trying to concentrate on questions about Kierkegaard with a doctoral student who had dropped by my office, and I told my daughter I would take her to the bathroom in just one second. But that second became a minute, and then she peed, right there on the floor. She was right. She did need to go to the bathroom. She was annoyed and defiant. I was ashamed. Mommy fail. Scholar fail. Pee-on-the-office-floor fail. I picked her up, told her not to be embarrassed, and ran out of the office toward the bathroom. As I left the office, a group of students were walking down the hallway. One of the men taking my class that semester shouted after me, "Remember Mother Julian!"

I suspect some readers have experienced settings that are fraught and competitive. In the university president's report on the status of women at Duke, released in 2003, women at every level of our own intricate hierarchy cited a pressure to perform "effortless perfection." And some of the most effective enforcers of this standard are other women, women who have been taught to pinch other women hard, under the arm, so that the bruise does not show unless you lift up your arm, risk further indignity, and show it to someone. I mean this figuratively, but it is an image that evokes horizontal violence in what is also a fairly cushy employment situation. If you believe your world is run by competition, scarcity, and proof of perfection, you may resort to forms of bullying that are subtle but effective in keeping the status quo. One colleague who is critical of this system calls this form of sisterly sabotage "matronizing." Reading and teaching Julian in the mix of this pressurized world of performance was a lifesaver to me. I recommend her as an antidote to any man or traitorous woman who tells you that you must lean in and give your soul to your workplace.

Here is another story from teaching Julian. In 2010 I was asked to give a named series of lectures about Julian at Point Loma University in California. The undergraduate students were required to attend, in a huge auditorium that seats a thousand people. Many of them sat toward the back. I am about 5'2" in heels, and I was not on the stage but on the floor. I was looking up into the balcony and trying to keep the students' attention. Julian was a hard sell to this almost exclusively evangelical Protestant student body. I am a woman, and I was lecturing on a lesser-known Catholic woman, whose handiest translation has on its cover a painting of a woman who looks to modern eyes like a Catholic nun. A student from the back row wanted to know how I could be sure about the truth of Julian's vision of God's abundance, given the fact of starvation. How could I affirm Julian's vision of God's goodness when all over the world people still deal with food shortages like the ones that caused thousands excruciating starvation in Julian's own time? On the way to give that lecture, I had stepped in a mess of freshly cooked mashed potatoes on the walkway. I had literally stepped in food that one of the students had dropped. So I talked about mashed potatoes, who has enough to spill, and who does not have anything. Famines, after all, are not only natural disasters. They are humanly constructed disasters, in part due to a way of thinking. This way of thinking is not about human beings as recipients of daily bread but about the mercantilist logic of markets.

Pope Francis made the news in November 20, 2014, when he told a gathering of world leaders that their economic systems exploit food as if it is just another commodity to be traded. Daily bread is not supposed to be exploited for financial gain. He called for food to be off-limits as a commodity open for speculation (that is, profit). While across two towns or two continents there are people without enough food—due to exploitative work patterns, industrialization, and the destruction of local agriculture—many of us who walk around schools like Duke and Point Loma have so much to eat we can drop food on the sidewalk. A vision of God's truth as Jesus's body given without reserve can be a vision that breaks open how you deem what is "realistic" about food. Julian's visions can be the truth that exposes the lie that there is not enough food for all of God's people to flourish.

Julian saw that God had kinned everyone and had become a servant so that we could know one another as one blood, drenched and saturated and fed by Jesus. Remember that Julian saw all of this when people like her were not supposed to receive the blood of Jesus at all, except metaphorically when the priest, set apart by station, received the blood for everyone else. She saw all of this kinship and abundance and enough-to-go-around in the middle of a time of exploitation and domination and division. This seeing of hers may be a redirection of vision. There are ways to deal with trauma that are primarily about survival. With versions of not-seeing, a person or a group of people can try not to see the alienating or brutal truth of what is happening to them. But there is another way of seeing that is not not-seeing but instead a redirection of vision. This can be individual, as when a person who has been abused learns over time to see flawed but basically kind people as worthy of trust. This can be corporate, as when a country that has suffered something like September 11, 2001, refuses perpetually to dwell on the possibilities of repetition or reprisal.

Julian's vision of at-one-ment is like a redirection of vision toward a truth that is sanguine in the best, original sense of that word. (More on that in chapter 3.) Julian describes her perspective on how a Christian can perceive herself in the world: "We should not on the one hand fall too low, inclining to despair, nor on the other hand be too reckless, as if we did not care, but should recognize our own weakness without concealment, knowing that we cannot stand even for the twinkling of an eye unless we are protected by grace. We should cling reverently to God, trusting in him alone; for man and God regard things in two quite different ways; it is proper for man humbly to accuse himself, and it is proper for God in his natural goodness kindly to excuse man" (LT: 52, 127).

This section of the Long Text is full of visual metaphors. Perceiving that God regards humans with the intent of gracious protection, Julian suggests that her readers observe themselves "without concealment." She means that I need not be afraid of God's view. God sees me, with kindness, and to receive that reassurance can be a loop back to my further transparency toward myself and toward God. There is no reason to bar God's view. Why? Because there is no hidden aspect of God that harbors accusation. This is key. God does not hide God's accusation until later, or until we finally come clean about our mess and our wounds. God transparently showed love through the atonement, joining Adam to Christ and joining us to the God-man. God invites trust, because Jesus's blood is more than sufficient to allow for open and honest appraisals of our uniquely beset and beautiful lives. Perceiving oneself with God's perception in mind may allow someone carrying deep shame to "cling reverently to God."

In the years after September 11, 2001, major media outlets swerved toward stories that fit a *Leave It to Beaver* family model, with a stable, heroic father and a resilient but dependent mother with children. Stories that did not fit were sometimes jammed into a box to try to make them fit, as with the story of a young military woman named Jessica Lynch or the story of female flight attendants taking on hijackers. Jessica

Lynch's story became a tale of a young victim of sexual assault rescued by military men. The courageous flight attendants were quickly overshadowed by a male hero who had shouted, "Let's roll!" The journalist Susan Faludi (2008) has written a helpful book called *The Terror Dream: Fear and Fantasy in Post–9/11 America* to try to sort out why this swerve happened; she suggests that 9/11 tore open a sense of shame within the culturally dominant American psyche. For people who thought their lives were safe from sheer tragic, intentional slaughter, the horrific spectacle worked. The reaction from major sources of media, as Faludi documents meticulously, was a kind of "cocooning" (her term). Whether or not most people wanted to go back underneath a safe blanket of nostalgic familiarity, that is where many television and radio stations went.

Faludi suggests that, after 9/11, stories that tap into a subterranean sense of shame and dread about feminine safety and masculine strength seemed compelling, or at least executives at major media outlets thought these stories about heroes and rescued damsels would hook people into keeping their eyeballs on a screen. Another journalist who has written on post–9/11 stories about marriages, women, and families in the media is Naomi Klein. In her book *The Shock Doctrine: The Rise of Disaster Capitalism*, Klein (2007) explains how powerful groups exploit disaster to manipulate people for the sake of various geopolitical goals. She details how the disorientation of a local or regional disaster can render people more susceptible to control by those trained in psychological tactics of coercion. Reading the two journalists together, I have come to believe (with other feminists) that there was a push by large media conglomerates to underscore a particular view of what counts as orderly during the decade after 9/11.

Households across the United States watched for days as scene after scene of unspeakable violence appeared on screens. Sounds of horror and of mourning came through car radios. These experiences seem to have elicited in some a sense of dread that is right up close to a sense of shame. Maybe one way to put this is to use that inappropriate but often used saying "We were caught with our pants down." Many people seem to have felt this way, only what happened to our naked undersides was not just embarrassment at being seen but violation. It is one thing to mourn the death of a loved one in relative isolation. On televisions and on radios across the country people were encouraged to experience over and over again a collective mourning that combined grief and dismay. This was not supposed to happen here. So, according to Faludi, some people were effectively pulled in by media outlets to watch or read stories of unequivocal, uncomplicated masculinity—stories of first responders as redemptive heroes and 9/11 widows as piously receptive to charity. It was one way to realign the universe so that the country could make sense of itself again.

Combining Klein's analysis with Faludi's is tricky. Both are trying to figure out how people have been controlled through images and reporting. But both also want to affirm that we, their readers, have the capacity to gain critical perspective on what they are describing. Their writing depends on our capacity to shake our heads and think differently. Teaching their work is also tricky, especially to gender-conservative and wholesome, trusting young students. Neither author takes great pains to be particularly winsome or apologetic toward students who have been taught to trust that mainstream media outlets and the default cultural rules of "normal" in the United States are basically good. Journalists in the United States do not have to choose each word with an eye toward a religious censor or a hangman's noose, and neither Faludi nor Klein targets readers who have been taught fundamentally to trust the authority figures in their world.

I find Julian helpful in thinking about these mundane pressures facing students. By the time Julian was expanding her Short Text into a Long Text, the crackdown on Christians who were asking questions in England had begun in earnest. Rules to reinforce the feudal hierarchy were building. In 1381 proponents of feudal reform took over the city of Norwich, and the bishop of Norwich, Henry le Despenser, helped lead an army of men to restore the usual order.

The peasant revolts during this period involved at least three intertwining refusals of the usual. Participants refused the church hierarchy, daring to go against what was presumed to be the divine ordering of the feudal system. One of the rhetorically loaded questions attributed to a rebel priest named John Ball, from the revolt of 1381, is "When Adam delved and Eve span, who was then the gentleman?" When Adam dug ditches for planting and Eve spun wool for clothing, they represented the origins of everyone on the earth. There were no "gentlemen" above them. Those who tried to turn the tables over in the peasant revolts refused the feudal hierarchy, daring to ignore the sorting system that declared men naturally ordered by blood to work or to master those who work. And they refused the military logic of their day. They acted in foolhardy ways, going against a systemic structure that had them outmanned, outgunned, and, well, out-everything. I find it a testimony to the power of these interlinked refusals that in only a few decades the archbishop of Canterbury would declare vernacular theology itself to be anathema, punishable by being publicly burned alive.

Julian is writing at this intersection of time, and she gently, consistently, carefully attests to an order of the universe that is different from the one written in stone all around her hearers and readers. She trusts that God can make a way through the visions she has received for people to receive also the capacity to gain critical perspective on the way of life reinforced by every liturgical and daily, domestic practice of her time. She has seen all that is held differently safe by God.

Dominant culture in the United States after 9/11 involves a nostalgic retrieval of a form of family. Stephanie Coontz (2000), an American historian, has helpfully given a term to this form of family in her book *The Way We Never Were: American Families and the Nostalgia Trap*. As she notes, the two parents, mom in pearls, dad happily employed 9 to 5, kids comically coming around to dad's wisdom at the end—that sort of "normal" family existed only on television in the 1950s. This is another way I find Julian's *Revelations of Divine Love* helpful for seeing the world around me. She did not dig into a version of order that told those dominated and ashamed around her to trust and obey the rules of her day. Her visions of God's love were what some readers might think of as maternal rather than commanding. Her revelations of God's power recalibrated the images of God's potency. God is sufficient to feed all of God's children during a time of such scarcity. God's humility is confounding—taking on our flesh in such a way that Jesus is identified as a servant. Julian saw this during a time when peasants were being chased by armies and mowed down like mice. God's way of counting is a noncounting. God does not reckon. God's saving blood spills over unaccountably. As Archbishop Rowan Williams (2000, 6) has written about grace in his book *The Wound of Knowledge*, "The only secure reality is something almost absurdly different, the anarchic mercy of God, which ignores order, rank and merit."

In one of her lessons about Holy Church and the importance of hearing the "preaching and teaching of Holy Church," Julian writes that "some mysteries are hidden from us because God wants them to be hidden," but sometimes we simply do not see the truth because we have not looked closely enough or trusted what we might see. When it comes to the mysteries that are not mysteries, God "wants to make them more open to us so that we may know him and love him and cling to him" (LT: 34, 88). After this Julian goes on to ask God about someone in particular whom she cares about, whether that person would cling to God.

I love it that Julian has just heard from God "All shall be well," but she then wants to make sure that God means it, by asking about someone whom she loves particularly: "And when almighty God had shown his great goodness so fully and so abundantly, I requested to know whether a certain person whom I loved would continue to lead a good life, as I hoped that she had already begun to do through God's grace. And in this personal request it seemed that I stood in my own way, for I was not answered immediately" (LT: 35, 89).

It is one thing to cross-stitch ALL SHALL BE WELL on a tea towel. But to believe it about someone I cannot imagine losing? That is another thing. God gives Julian an answer that is slightly confusing at first. God tells her not to focus on "any particular thing" but to "consider him in all things" (LT: 35, 89). This could sound as if she is supposed to see everyone and everything through a blurry haze of trust. Instead, however, she seems to have learned that, by seeing God "in an instant," she can stop obsessing over the daily struggles of someone she loves. She writes, "For by the same power, wisdom and love with which he made all things, our good Lord is continually leading all things to the same end and he himself shall bring this about" (35, 89).

This way of seeing the truth is not about blurring the lines of particularity. This way of seeing the truth can bring into delicate relief the specificity of all that God has made, including those we love most. A contemporary of Denise Levertov is the poet Vassar Miller. They have different styles, though both wrote poems about their bodies and about God. Miller (1991, 164) has a poem that whimsically makes clear how perspicacious our vision of truthfulness can become in the mix of grace; it is called "Delayed Gratitude" and appears in a collection of her poems entitled *If I Had Wheels or Love*:

Become the friends of small things, I take
crickets and gnats for topic,
even the ant arched by my dog's armpit,
for whom I will write an epic

and thereby give him a voice which none
ever did for the ant,
even the Lord who made vocal chords,
creation somewhat aslant.

But he shall surely speak through my verses,
(you can like it or lump it)
The ant no child hears with ears still magic.
My poem shall prove his trumpet.

For he earns it, he and every other
animated caprice,
to me even their limited warfare
being a gesture of peace.

Seeing the tiny details of this world around you as animated and miraculously capricious—or whimsically surprising—is part of a truth that may make you seem strange. As Miller words it here, in a "creation somewhat aslant" seeing poetically may allow one to see each particular small thing as an "animated caprice" of that very creator. Seeing creatively, with Julian of Norwich, may allow one to perceive a "gesture of peace" even where struggle and competition seem to be the rule of all that is. People who see the creatures and people around them only as things to be measured and assessed and evaluated and sold will think you are wasting your time if you see in this way. People who see competition and scarcity written into the natural world will think you are besotted to find in ants a "gesture of peace." So be it. Let them be confused.

Spiritual Safety

> The beauty and vividness of the blood are like nothing but
> itself. It is as plentiful as the drops of water which fall from
> the eaves after a heavy shower of rain, drops which fall so
> thickly that no human mind can number them. . . . And
> this was what gave me most happiness and the strongest
> sense of spiritual safety.
>
> —JULIAN OF NORWICH, *Revelations of Divine Love*

During the initial outbreak and recurrences of the Great Plague, local pastors responsible for praying with dying people before they died were some of the most likely to die themselves. You cannot administer the last rites wearing a hazmat suit, throwing prayers at someone from across the room. The last rites require touching people on the forehead, helping them take in the body of Jesus, the bread, though they may be nearly unable to take in anything. Although people at the time did not know precisely why the plague was spreading so quickly, it was clear that physical proximity was a part of the macabre disaster. And as people quickly succumbed to the disease, vomiting blood was a horrible part of a person's death. To receive, as an image of safety, blood spilling "as plentiful as the drops of water which fall from the eaves after a heavy shower of rain" (LT: 7, 51) was to receive a different world than the world that other adults in Julian's generation had grown up dreading.

In addition to the plague, many of the same people had heard about or watched men and women fighting for reform of the brutal feudal system slain like lambs to a slaughter. For human blood to be a sign of spiritual safety was a not a different answer to the same, usual question of evil, but a different question and a different answer. Where was God in the blood spilled senselessly after the peasants failed to counter the armies of the lords? Where was God in the bloody horror of the plague that had left loved ones dead? Julian received a redirection away from an accounting of God. I find this to be not a denial of evil but a redefinition of how to see one another within and after a display of regional tragedy and domination. Jesus's blood is uncountable, plentiful, profligate, and more than sufficient to soak the cursed ground and to reach those who had died without receiving the last rites. The unshriven dead and the massacred rebels are uncountable, and the blood to save them is without reserve.

Recall that Watson and Jenkins (2006, 3) write that Julian's longer text "is a work with no real precedent" and that she had written a "speculative vernacular theology" that is "structured as a prolonged investigation into the divine." Julian's "investigation into the divine" goes through the central focus of the bloody cross, and Jesus's blood at-ones people. The proper word for what she had seen in her visions is *sanguine*. The word means both bloody red and having a disposition to see the world with hopeful confidence. She is seeing securely through the blood red of a reality different from the bloody realism of violence, retribution, death, and destruction. Julian is sanguine about time, the truth, and our bodies. Seeing through the cross, she writes, "The love of God unites us to such an extent that when we are truly aware of it, no man can separate himself from another" (LT: 65, 150). God "can do all that is necessary for us," that is, "love, longing, and pity." This "longing" pulls us toward God, and God's longing, or "thirst," for us pulls "mankind in general up into himself" (75, 164). Julian does not mean that God draws "mankind" as a giant blob of personhood or as a generalized concept into himself. God draws each person together, toward God and kinned, or at-oned in blood through Jesus. The term "mankind in general," which she uses here, she has specified earlier in her text as "all who shall be saved," or, in Middle English, "alle that shalle be safe" (36, 92; Watson and Jenkins 2006, 358). Her "investigation into the divine," then, is "vernacular" in a radical, at-the-root sense of that word. She investigates God for the sake of people who were considered at this time, by official theologians and by most people within the aristocracy, merely a mass of a generalizable class. She writes for the uncountable group of people, counted only when taxed or possibly when baptized or registered as dead. Julian writes with an attention to our being kinned, stitched together with God's blood-red thread.

It is as if Julian's visions swirl the feudal system together into a funnel that mixes everyone up so that no one can distinguish lord from lady from farmer from king from prince from priest from orphan left at the monastery from monk to nun. That does not mean everyone becomes a human mush of general humanness. People are kinned in a way that has us seeing one another as people with particularity instead of as groups of people with carefully calculated qualifications or lack of power. God has redirected her vision to show us that the question of who is "worth knowing" and who is not is the wrong question for our holy lives. We are all known and pulled together toward the one who wants to save each one of us.

One of the undergraduate students I taught in a science and humanities class gave me permission to retell a story she told me about her work with mice. The seminar she had taken with me her first year at Duke was not within the divinity school, and she herself is not Christian. One of the purposes of the course was to have students question the ways that definitions of progress quantify people or turn them into machines that merely do things rather than live. We looked at the eugenics movement in the United States as well as how standardized testing has shaped education. Several years after the seminar, when she was preparing for graduate school, she told me about her experience taking mice out of a cage to register their activity. She was responsible for noting when each mouse had been born, when the mouse had been taken out of the cage for experimentation, and when the mouse had died. What had struck her so much in the gut were the times when she noted that a mouse had only a date of birth and a date of death. Many of the mice had never been out of the cage. "Dr. Hall," she told me, "sometimes I feel like one of those mice."

The grinding system of work this young woman experienced is, I contend, formally similar to the way that Christian practices can function during a political regime like the one during Julian's time. What Christians in charge during Julian's lifetime were most responsible for was to register births (or baptisms) and register deaths (or funerals) and otherwise, in between birth and death, to make sure people stayed within the established order. Christian life in between birth and death was partly about staying inside one's assigned cage of thought and practice. Julian's visions counter this world with a different power than an assembled army of rebels. She investigates the divine and finds there the vernacular truth of Christianity. A meaning of the word *vernacular* involves a notion of what is "natural" or "native" to people who speak to one another in a particular region. Julian found in her investigation of God that the feudal system—a system wherein people who speak neither Latin nor French are like mice—is not at all natural. What is natural is holy consanguinity.

Another example may help explain the import of Julian's vision of blood flowing, unaccountable and plentiful, as during a steady rain. When I was in college I heard a lecture about bears barfing up human limbs. I have searched in vain to figure out exactly which medieval historian came to speak at Emory University around 1988 to talk about Western European depictions of the days right before heaven, when each of us becomes re-membered and brought to God. She was brilliant and from someplace like Harvard, and I was sure from that year on that I liked church history. The historian showed us a slide of a painting from some time before individual portraits were all the rage. The painting was vast and detailed, with many different scenes going on at once. It showed a large fish barfing up a whole person, a bear with an arm coming out of its mouth, and all sorts of other carnivorous animals coughing up heads and hands and arms and feet. (This is from memory, mind you, but you get the idea.) She explained to us that the problem of what would happen to our bodies when we each and all finally go to heaven, in bodily form, as Jesus does in the resurrection, was quite alive and distressing during the many centuries when people had actually been eaten by and defecated out by predators and scavengers all over the adjacent forest or in the nearby sea.

What stayed with me was just how bizarre belief in the resurrection of each individual body is. I remember thinking that Paul of Tarsus was right to say that unless we believe in Jesus Christ both crucified and risen, we might as well be something other than Christian. (That is a paraphrase of Paul, of course.) The second weirdest thing that people who follow Jesus believe is that God does not count awards or place on the totem pole of any hierarchy as anything to be bothered with. And the first weirdest thing that Christians believe is that all of those people swirled together are going to be individually resurrected and eating together, someday, beyond any way we can predict. We will be both different and individual and awkwardly together someday. Scripture says not only will the lion barf up the lamb, but each lion and lamb will be friends in heaven.

The swirl of dismembered body parts that is an airline disaster or genocide or a village ravaged by a tiger is not beyond God. I find this both confusing and desperately compelling. The vision of the last days when each of us will be at a heavenly banquet with God is not what I would call reassurance. The word *reassurance* seems wrong. Reassurance in the middle of misery is invasive, like a commercial break for bubble bath in the middle of a documentary about the trench warfare of World War I. Unless you have a thick and enduringly lizard-like skin, reckoning with suffering while saying "God will provide" seems either stupid or cruel or under the influence of deadening pharmaceuticals. Watching people rage and weep over the non-sense that is a tragic or effectively manipulated loss still renders me speechless. But turning again to Julian's visions has helped me to think about what it means that I still keep arguing, and hoping, that what Julian saw is true. I want someday to laugh at the Devil and at the carnival that is all of us being barfed up individually, re-membered by God, and celebrating together.

Here is one thing Julian does not specify, but that I am inspired by her to specify: I think the turned-upside-down vision that Julian received suggests that, in heaven, the lamb tells the lion where to sit. And the previously eaten lamb can tell the lion to sit far away from her and learn for a few decades how to be a vegetarian, before the lion is allowed to speak to the lamb. Julian's vision is like magic, and it is a redirection about time. But any lamb with any sense will want to make sure that heaven does not involve her quivering with fear that the lion might just forget she is now in an entirely different reality from the one so aptly described by Tennyson as "red in tooth and claw." The vision of heaven that Julian received is not the present mess, spiffed up merely to appear eternally peaceful.

I have waited until now to explain an important part of Julian's world. She also lived during a time when people were not sure who was in charge of what, from king to king, prince to prince, lord to lord, and, most ominously, from pope to pope. Her vision of Holy Church may be the hardest vision to swallow for some Protestant readers. In the middle of all the various crises of ecclesial authority, brought on by brazenly open power struggles within western Europe, Julian affirmed that Jesus is still one body. She affirms, without an asterisk, that the Holy Church is both Mother and whole. She affirms in her writing that the Mother Church is not broken, no matter the machinations of the various men attempting to use Christianity to shift or consolidate their power:

And he wants us to cling strongly to the faith of Holy Church and find our dearest Mother there in the comfort of true understanding with the whole blessed community; for a single person may often feel broken, but the whole body of Holy Church has never been broken, nor ever shall be, for all eternity. And therefore it is a safe, good and gracious thing to wish humbly and strongly to be supported by and united to our mother, Holy Church, that is Christ Jesus; for there is plenty of the food of mercy which is his dearest blood and precious water to make us clean and pure.

(LT: 61, 144)

In this passage Julian does a trick with the words *broken* and *food* and *blood*. From 1378 to 1418 the Roman Catholic Church went through what historians now call the Papal Schism or the Western Schism. There were two popes vying for authority and connection to multiple factions across western Europe capable of waging war to gain more land. During the same period England (whose Christian practice was still Roman Catholic) went through its usual breaking apart and reassembling, with challenges to the throne by both righteous, murderous peasants and ambitious, murderous contesters. The capital "C" Church was both bloody and verifiably broken. But Julian uses the same words—*church, blood,* and *broken*—to mean a different thing.

Popes will come and go. Lords will lord their power over one another and anyone who challenges them. Kings will declare themselves, divorce their cousins, and proclaim their ability to protect their people from other people. Julian asserts that this unreality is not the really real. She has her reader consider the way a "single person" may feel in her life often "broken," and focuses on this problem. The person who finds herself broken is "broken" in a way that does indeed matter in the divine scheme of things. The "single person" may "often feel broken," and, in Julian's time, the signs of brokenness of other "single persons" were not subtle. Individuals with power could not only display their brokenness but could break others around them. And, living with fear and hunger, individuals without power may have, as today, found themselves tempted to break another person, perhaps family members or neighbors or people working for them, controlling at least some aspect of their lives that seemed so thoroughly under the control of others above them in the structures that kept people obedient. There was every reason to see the world divided. And there were official voices declaring the world whole, intact, and under the control of the same individuals who were breaking people and regions and the Church. Julian's vision allows her to commend the Holy Church as a mother who remains whole and safe. That Mother Church is full of mercy, blood, and water for all of her children. This is the safety she sees.

What might all of this mean for real churches, for real people who meet to worship God in buildings on street corners or in shopping malls today? In the *United Methodist Hymnal*, the Apostles' Creed, an affirmation of faith that many Western Christians use in their church services, has a footnote next to the words "holy catholic church." Methodists affirm the holy catholic church with small "h," small "c," and small "c," and the footnote indicates this means "universal." Just to make sure, we are reminded we do not "affirm" or "believe in" the Holy Catholic Church.

There are well-worn jokes about the divisions and differences between kinds of churches. Methodists are Baptists who read. Episcopalians are Catholics who use birth control. Lutherans are Catholics who go to college. Presbyterians are Methodists who run for Congress. Many of the jokes in each region of the United States are more about social class than about substantive, doctrinal differences. And then there is the often repeated fact about Christianity in this country: that the hour during which Christians worship God is the most racially segregated hour of our lives. Is it crazy to hear Julian say that Mother Church is unbroken and a place of real sustenance for any single, broken individual?

One of my favorite quotes about the strangeness of this affirmation of "one holy catholic church" comes from a biography of St. Augustine of Hippo. The writer, a historian named James O'Donnell (2006, 174), words the weirdness just right: "The notion that what one sees today on an evangelist's television program, in the cave monasteries of the Pechersk Lavra in Kiev, and in an African cathedral welcoming a papal visit, to say nothing of an upper Manhattan Episcopalian Sunday service regularly attended by house pets and their owners, are all of a piece with what happened in Augustine's lifetime in the Syrian desert, in farming villages in Africa, and among perfumed socialites in Rome is to make a quite extraordinary theological assertion in the guise of history." I do not know O'Donnell's story or what is at stake for him in telling with such accuracy the distinct differences between the realities of worshipers in such disparate settings. But I do know that many people who reject Christianity outright have been wounded by precisely the faith that is supposed to be balm. If you walk into a church, there should be a balm in that Gilead. I have had students and beloved friends who are spiritual but not practically religious because Christianity has been used as an instrument of shame or division or coercion or outright abuse. In addition to the usual horrible historical reasons to stay away from a church—the Crusades, Christian complicity in the Holocaust, slavery in the United States—there are arguably some good reasons right at this moment to stay way far away from television evangelism, a monastery, a papal visit, or, for that matter, a Manhattan Episcopalian Sunday service. Someone near to me was told by a well-meaning but clueless leader of a parachurch organization that her doubts about God were a sign that the Devil was tempting her. She was, fact be noted, dealing with a situation of abuse, and Christianity was used back at her as an accusation, and a cause for nightmares later. What child of God needs to hear that her doubts are proof that the embodiment of evil is right there, over her shoulder, tempting her? Another example is the recurring message that people made by God to be fearfully and wonderfully gay or lesbian can twist their bodies and souls into being not gay or lesbian, either through self-punishing "therapy" or, as the newest theory goes, by embracing the fluidity of gender, entering a heterosexual marriage and finding ways to stay married by thinking of gender identity as sufficiently fluid to sustain it. (This is a newly sophisticated way to use feminist theory to advance an antigay form of Christianity.)

Julian has helped me to see that the whole, intact body of what she calls Holy Church is not a matter of history or empirical evidence. Belief in Holy Church is a matter of avowal. If you put Jesus's blood to the test, under a microscope, it will be a drop of grape juice, fermented or unfermented. If you put Jesus's body, Holy Church, to the test, it will involve a long and detailed list of abuses of power, from small-time cruelties that went unreported to large-scale cover-ups that, thank God, are now being reported. What Julian seems to say to the unreality of human sin written into the fabric of her beloved Christianity in England is that this unreality is there but not the definitive word. When Julian laughs at the Devil, she is also laughing at the presumptions of dueling popes and princes and lords. She is naming the use of Christianity for the sake of power as the worst foolishness. She names the whole bloody "truth" as a nonsensical pageant of lies.

The hard part for me, and for many others who see the bloody truth in front of us, is that she also says, all things being counted, there is an unaccountable *there* in the cup of salvation. In this cup, held with hands that upheld the patriarchal despotism that was turn-of-the-century England, is the blood of Christ. She is able to say this in part because God came to her, in a vision, and gave her the blood of Jesus right straight into her body and being. In effect the blood of Christ is ow hers. She has imbibed the profuse, plentiful blood of Jesus and now sees that blood of Jesus where it is hiding in plain sight: in the empirically corrupt Church and the churches of her and our time. Holy Church is not broken. It is our source of safety.

The fact that Christianity is not a matter of facts makes Christian faith a potentially stupefying brew. Christianity can be used to distract people from what is happening to them or around them. Dismissing atheists and nonpracticing believers of various sorts in the United States as selfish or deluded or whatever other accusation churchgoers might want to pitch across the church wall at them misses that many people who believe in God avoid going to church because they have seen churches dope people into ignoring the bloody truth of the world around them.

I have many friends and family members who cannot stand churches for this reason. I myself have struggled to make myself go to worship

God on Sundays, putting one foot in front of the other much more under the force of determined habit than with joy. So I want to think about Julian's words on Mother Church and the blood and the bloody truth of evil. Julian's affirmation of the wholeness of Holy Church and her unqualified confirmation that the blood of Jesus is truly there in the cup at the Lord's Supper or Communion (or Mass)—these are examples of an avowal. Julian avows, or makes a confession of belief, about what she sees to be true about the sustained unbrokenness of Mother Church.

I learned a word a few years ago that describes well a psychological coping mechanism I have seen in my two decades of working as a pastor-scholar. That word is *disavowal*. It means something subtly different from outright denial. Denial is a form of not seeing at all. Disavowal is a way of actively trying not to see a truth about someone or something you love. Disavowal is sometimes aided by alcohol or drugs (legal or illegal) and sometimes by other means of distraction. I have seen and I have experienced the danger of being a Christian who disavows the bloody truth of bad unreality in front of my eyes.

To deny is somehow to be able not to see at all. To disavow is to see evil but try somehow not to reckon with the reality of what this evil entails. I have listened to people whose faith involves their disavowal of evil. I have seen this when a man needed to face and eventually celebrate that God created him beautifully and wonderfully gay. I have seen this when a woman needed to tell her lover that she is worth more than being used as an unpaid therapist under the covers. I have seen this when a man with a life sentence tries to endure with dignity the spectacle that is coercion and domination in a high-security prison. I have seen this when a woman has faced either leaving the sisters she loves or stating that the Christian community they help to legitimate is an elaborate cult of lies.

Disavowal can be deadly, and Christianity can become intertwined with an unreality that looks close to the reality of faithful truth. In his recent book on Julian's theology, Denys Turner (2011) thinks of Julian alongside the writings of Dante, who lived and wrote about God shortly before Julian lived and wrote. Turner's section on their similar understandings of sin is helpful on what Julian avows and how her visions are not an example of disavowal:

> If we are to say that sin is a *refusal of reality*, this does not mean that it is in any way an *unreal refusal*, for to say that to live in sin is to live within illusion is by no means the same as to say that sin is illusory. Refusing reality can have every sort of real consequence, can cause every sort of pain and suffering, can weave warps and webs of fantasy and illusion, can create and sustain whole regimes of deceit, can motivate personalities distorted by such fears and self-deceptions so as to generate all the world's violence, all the world's need for it, and all the world's untold numbers of cruelties—all of which can join up into interlocked systems, into self-sustaining structures, which conspire to be a world made out of the material of its unreality. . . . Of course, then, sin is real, and there is nothing in Julian's theology that would suggest otherwise. But her saying that sin is "real" is perfectly consistent with her also saying that sin has "no substance, no manner of being." . . . Sin is real in the sense that an unreality can become the real substance of a person's or of a society's existence, a kind of *really lived refusal of the real*. (94–95, italics in the original)

Sin, for Julian, can become a "really lived refusal of the real." I would add, and I think Turner would consider this compatible with his reading, that my "really lived refusal of the real" can be particularly tenacious if my naming this unreality as unreal requires me to question the faith that I have been taught. If the "self-sustaining structures" of a mendacious form of Christianity have been for me a splint against the impending chaos of life, I may find it almost impossible to release my desperate grasp on this form of faith. If my particular community or practice of Christianity is intertwined with untruth, I may find it unthinkable to think in any different way. Put simply, evil is particularly hard for some Christians to face if that evil is intertwined with a version of Christian language or Christian practice that seems inextricably part of faith.

The biggest crisis of my own faith came when I had to try to trust again in the goodness of Jesus on the cross after realizing, finally, that I had been using the cross, subconsciously, as a reason to stay in a marriage that was dissolving my soul into oblivion. I had to find a way to shake my head clear of disavowal, state where the cross had become untruth for me, and receive another way back, through grace, to see the cross as my at-one-ment with God. This is not a success story but an ongoing one. Julian's visions have been for me a way to receive the truth that the cross is not a trick. But even testifying that Christianity can be dangerous has been a challenge for some neighbors and students to hear. If Christianity is your splint, hearing that it can also be subtly, almost imperceptibly sick or untrue or destructively illogical can lead you, perhaps, to turn all of your most defensive mechanisms against the messenger.

Some people need faith to be psychologically reliable. I have felt that. I need to know that Christian faith will measurably save me from a hurt that makes my soul suffer. Some people need Christian faith to be historically reliable. I have known that. I have wanted to know that, just because some fake shroud or relic or newly found ancient scroll seems to discount Jesus as the Christ, there is another shroud or scroll or relic (or scholar who can interpret any of those things) that makes my faith in Jesus Christ historically reliable and legitimate. Some Christians require their faith to be analytically reliable. I have not myself known this particular desire because math made virtually no sense to me after Algebra II, and no one who taught me math could tolerate all my questions. I gave up on math long ago as a beacon of existential truth. But in all of these ways, the *hard-held-heart-need* for Christianity to be solid and fully functional as a system of intertwined truthful truths has led some people to disavow the fact that Christianity has been used in ways that are deeply wrong. The desire to defend my own faith can lead me to disavow the fact that the words of Christianity have been and are still used in ways that are intertwined with evil itself.

Julian looked the bloody truth in the face. She received the grace not to disavow, and she trusted that grace and kept searching, investigating God with the trust that God would not be offended by her questions. What chutzpah does that take for a woman, during a time when women were not supposed to learn how to talk about theology? What does it mean to have such moxie? I am trying to learn.

Advice a friend gave me in the mix of my own maelstrom of faith and doubt was to be my "own best mother." This sounded so clichéd at the time that I did not trust anything else she said for a while. For the next month I walked my dogs and washed lots of dishes and graded lots of papers. And two weeks later this friend was again in my head. "My own best mother." It clicked. I should be the best mother to myself that I would want my daughters to be to themselves.

I can make better sense of being my own best mother while reading Julian. One of the passages from *Revelations of Divine Love* that has stayed with me over fifteen years is this one:

> The blessed wounds of our Saviour are open and rejoice to heal us; the sweet, gracious hands of our Mother are ready and carefully surround us; for in all this he does the work of a kind nurse who has nothing to do but occupy herself with the salvation of her child. His task is to save us, and it is his glory to do so, and it is his wish that we know it; for he wants us to love him tenderly, and trust him humbly and strongly. And he showed this in these gracious words, "I hold you quite safely." (LT: 61, 144)

Julian likens Jesus to a mother and to a "kind nurse," layering two images of actual, physical care. In their commentary on this passage Watson and Jenkins (2006, 317) note that Julian evokes the image of Jesus as taking on "the same employment of an actual nurse" and that her words about "the salvation of her child" (in the Spearing translation) is an even "yet humbler image for Christ's care of the soul, since a nurse might be a paid professional." The text in Julian's original English is helpful here: "For he, in alle this werking, useth the very office of a kinde nurse, that hath not elles to done but to entende about the salvation of her childe" (317). Jesus's work is much like that of a nurse, she writes, like a nurse who is also like a mother who has nothing else to do but stay attentive to the care of her child. While an actual mother may have many things to do that are not directly focused on the care of one particular child in a household, Julian layers the image of mother with that of a focused nurse who is appointed specifically to care for one particular child. This vision underlines what she has said about church in this same section (LT: 61). It may appear as if God has forsaken particular people, given the divisions within the church, but God shows Julian that each person is held, safely, as if by a mother with only focused love in mind.

One medievalist suggested to me that the word *nurse* here is most akin to someone who serves as an orderly in a hospital, caring for the body of someone who is physically vulnerable. Both orderlies and mothers generally have to deal with blood. Modern-day surgeons do too, but they mostly try to go around the blood and stitch together parts of the body that are solid, not liquid. Surgeons work as brilliant engineers of the body. Orderlies serve in a different sort of role. Blood is unpredictable, flows, and has to be cleaned up. Blood today, in a world of contagion, is also potentially contaminated. As I write, another round of fear has torn through the Western media, as people have been inundated by words on our screens about and images of the danger of blood coming across the border to bring a new plague. Julian writes that the "blessed wounds" are open in a way that heals us. She writes that a Mother is powerfully ready to surround us, and links this all to open wounds. She writes that Jesus is prepared to save us, "tenderly."

How is Jesus's blood sweet, when the distinction between bloodlines was what supposedly divided people from one another? How was Jesus's blood poured out unaccountably a source of safety, when blood and vomit were part of the recurring devastation of death by disease? Bringing this out of the fluid and into the material reality of power in health care today, how does a woman affirm that God is like a "kind nurse" when an orderly is not customarily the obvious broker of power in the worldly scheme of things? Julian called Jesus a nurse and a mother at a time when, much like my own time, it would have sounded more powerful to call Jesus a "doctor" and a "father." Reading Julian in a way that crisscrosses the questions of her visions then and the questions of her seeing now helps to illuminate what is so beautifully strange about her visions of God's love. It is God's "glory" to be a mother and an orderly who occupies himself with the safety of each particular child in the pediatric ward.

I have had trouble explaining to students why it is not a bad crazy to believe against what I call the pragmatism of reckoned power. The futility of playing a power game to climb any ladder of hierarchy dawned on me early in life. This requires some personal detail. I read Machiavelli's calculation of power in all its forms—interpersonal, generational, and international—when I was in college. I was eighteen, and I was experiencing for the first time since before adolescence a real taste of what felt like success, not only with good grades but also, most palpably, by acting a lead part on a stage. Performing on stage with all of my inhibitions channeled toward getting the part right, I experienced what felt like power. I had felt that power for the first time on stage as Linus's sister, Lucy, in my elementary school's performance of *You're a Good Man, Charlie Brown*. That was in fourth grade, and I had (as remembered by my totally objective mother) rocked the house with my unabashed voice. Then puberty hit, and the bishop moved my family to a small city in West Texas with totally different rules.

I stayed mostly obedient and cowed until I left home to attend college far away in Atlanta. My first semester at Emory University I landed the role of Sandy in the Emory performance of *Grease*. This is a play that became a hit movie when I was about ten, and I was giddy with the glow of success. The play is grittier than the movie; the script suggests Sandy has been moved to a different school because she became pregnant at her previous school. The Hollywood version of Sandy features an Australian who has all the physical attributes of a blonde ingénue. My first year at Emory I was newly a nonvirgin, and I played alongside unapologetically worldly young women in their junior and senior years. I was smitten again with theater. Here were college women who smoked cigarettes and did not care what people thought of their boyfriends. They helped me find my moxie again. By playing Sandy

I shed my shame of having had premarital sex with my high school senior sweetheart. I made the dean's list both semesters that year, in no small part because I rediscovered my self-confidence. All this may sound saccharine to readers who did not grow up in a Christian household, but for generations of young women in the United States, even after birth control was widely available, sexual "purity" was the marker of power. To see our bodies and brains otherwise required of many of us a total shift in perspective.

My sophomore year at Emory I also discovered political science. I started reading every book of political theory I could afford at the local bookstores. Machiavelli in particular fascinated me. He seemed so realistic and true about how the world works. I had interned in a law office my first summer out of college and so had been given a glimpse of the mess that is legal pragmatism in the Wild West. San Angelo, Texas, in the 1980s was not so different from middle Europe during Machiavelli's time. I thought I had found my mentor for life's way. Perhaps consider this my Ayn Rand moment, although, thank God, we did not read her at Emory. One weekend while at a work-study job, trying to write an essay overdue for a political science class, I turned to a section in which Machiavelli says something or other about "woman." Until that point, reading voraciously, I had counted myself the advisee to Machiavelli's advice. Then I realized I was not his advisee. I was the woman who could be used as another pawn in the great chess game of life that was and still is pragmatism.

I might feel a sense of power dancing on stage and gain a few charges of real power with every "A" on my transcript at a prestigious university like Emory. But something clicked in me after I had read Western political thought, from Aristotle to Hobbes to Marx. If I wanted truly to identify with women, I needed to think differently than with the calculus of accruing power. Machiavelli wrote a century or so after Julian, a few regions away, but still in the wake of the wars of religion, crises of power and authority, hunger, and recurrences of the plague. Julian is as wise as a serpent and as innocent as a dove. Machiavelli is as wise as a serpent and as alluring as a dove cooked in wine sauce. Julian's answer to the raw and dehumanizing power struggles going on around her was to reject the going definitions of *crazy* and *sane*.

In my attempt to explain to students why I refuse to be sane in a baffling world, I have also quoted Prince's 1984 classic "Let's Go Crazy." In the song he invites his "dearly beloved" to "get through this thing called life" by looking around at one another and finding friendship. It is "nuts," he notes, to find love more possible than fear. The song came out during the mid-1980s era of Ronald Reagan and the high heat of the cold war. This era included nuclear bombs in the USSR aimed at the United States and in the United States aimed at the USSR. Three years after "Let's Go Crazy" became a hit, a group called R.E.M. came out with a song called "It's the End of the World as We Know It (And I Feel Fine)." The daily national, secular magazine news during the late 1980s in the United States was about apartheid in South Africa or about bloody, chaotic civil wars throughout the areas caught in the cross fire of the two warring superpowers. The grown-ups around me who paid attention to world politics either seemed despondent or else assured me from their own form of pragmatism that something called "mutually assured destruction" was going to save me and my generation from the nuclear apocalypse. The USSR was not going to obliterate the United States, so the idea went, because the USSR would be obliterated, almost simultaneously, by the United States. My friends and I tried to make light of this by noting that the political doctrine keeping us "safe" was known by the acronym MAD. But if we were reading the news carefully, and some of us were, we knew that people caught between the two superpowers were being tortured and starved and bombed and manipulated by each gigantic war-mongering system of governance. Both superpowers involved in MAD were stomping on human beings between the two continents.

What goes around comes back around, and my daughters are now watching a new form of supposed containment of foreign chaos through the security of drone strikes in other countries and surveillance cameras on every street corner in their hometown. Seeing the world with Julian may be close to going nuts with ecstatic, unself-conscious friendship, fueled by faith instead of drugs, during a period when young people are being told either to be afraid or to check out—or both. How does the bread of the Lord's Supper become Jesus? How do the squashed grapes become Jesus? To believe that these bits of material things that are also commonplace are truly Jesus is to be a bit nuts and to be invited into a nonpragmatic space of safety.

Revelations of Divine Love accepts neither apocalyptic fervor nor mystical escape from the mundane. The fact that Jesus has become flesh means that we hold little things big and big things small. If everything that is is God's loving extravagance, held like a hazelnut, this can free me from succumbing to the tactics of fear and division. Julian writes, "On the one hand he wants us to know that he does not only concern himself with great and noble things, but also with small, humble, and simple things, with both one and the other; and this is what he means when he says, 'All manner of things shall be well': for he wants us to know that the smallest things shall not be forgotten" (LT: 32, 85).

The small things have not been lost and will not be forgotten by God. How do we dance into that song? There are many pop songs about going temporarily crazy for someone you desire sexually. Those can be fun. I will not hate on songs about being smitten with another precious child of God. Going nuts for another person other than Jesus can be a truly beautiful gift. (I will say more about that love in chapter 4.) The nuts that Julian recommends is about seeing the entire world in a way that kins us, through blood, to one another. And the source of that kinship, Julian avers, is Mother Church, which remains unbroken, all signs to the contrary. It is there, through that best mother, that we receive truly the blood of Jesus. This is the crazy for God's love. This is the safety created by God in Jesus Christ, as each of us are held, unforgotten, tended to as if by a mother with no other work than to love us.

BODIES
Nakedly and Truly

> Think hard too about the deep significance of this word
> "ever"; for it was a great sign of the love he shows in our
> salvation, with the numerous joys that follow from the
> Passion of Christ; one is that he rejoices that he has indeed
> done it, and he will suffer no more; another, that he has
> brought us up to heaven and made us his crown and his end-
> less delight; another is that he has by this means bought us
> from the endless torments of hell.
>
> —JULIAN OF NORWICH, *Revelations of Divine Love*

Jesus "rejoices" that "he has indeed done it" and will "suffer no more." Because the Fiend has been overcome, we may cheer ourselves by laughing at the Fiend himself. Julian also says that in her vision Jesus did not laugh at the Devil. Yet Jesus wants us to laugh. He wants us to be free and brave and not part of the public humiliation he endured alone. I read this part of Julian's vision as a testimony that Jesus's sacrifice is not to be repurposed for yet another political agenda, either during her time or during my own. What Jesus suffered is not to be suffered by anyone else as part of God's work of salvation.

This is what I call the nonproductivity of the cross. Grace is not a dose of political moxie that allows me to keep suffering for a cause, with an eye toward the measurable ways that Jesus Christ is causing an uptick in political progress toward a discernible goal. In the words of my colleague and friend Stan Goff, this is what makes my reading of Julian nonprogressive. She has received a bodily experience of Jesus's suffering in a way that cannot be described as useful to any think tank or cause. Julian is useful like daily bread is useful—not to be hoarded and counted. If I try counting with the methods of data the ways Jesus is accomplishing something in my life or my community, that daily bread of grace grows mold. With this image I am drawing on a story from Exodus 16, when God's people are told to accept daily bread and not hoard it. The form of hoarding in my corner of the professional-academic-Christian world has less to do with accumulating stuff than with trying to accumulate numbers—of people, of funding, of clicks on an article or purchases of a book—to verify that God is actually doing something through me and through my reception of grace. I think Julian's visions redirect me away from this new form of hoarding, warning me not to allow myself to be tempted to make anyone's suffering count.

Jesus knows human suffering and can be a part of human suffering because he took on everything we have ever endured or have hidden. One way into what Julian means about how Jesus Christ united himself with all who suffer is with two classic songs from the United States that draw from John Steinbeck's classic American novel *The Grapes of Wrath*. Steinbeck's character Tom Joad inspired both Woody Guthrie and Bruce Springsteen to write songs about the invisible, merely potential, but sometimes palpable connection between people who have been counted as nothing and yet resist being treated as nothing. Guthrie's song "Tom Joad" ends:

Wherever little children are hungry and cry,
Wherever people ain't free.
Wherever men are fightin' for their rights,

That's where I'm a-gonna be, Ma.
That's where I'm a-gonna be.

Steinbeck, Guthrie, and Springsteen wrote into their words a reckoning with what Jesus might have meant when he told the disciples that he himself is present when the hungry are hungry and the thirsty gasp for water. This passage, known by many of my students as the "least of these" passage, is often interpreted as a warning to those who have plenty of food and do not give it to people who are hungry. Guthrie's words take a different perspective from within this story. Rather than having disciples or would-be disciples know themselves as called to give, the song implores the hearer to know Jesus is with the people who are currently in bondage, in famine, or under the rule of someone who counts them as worthless. The song says that Jesus is with those who are suffering and also struggling no longer to have to bear the suffering inflicted on them by the most-of-these.

Julian sees that "just as the Holy Trinity made all things from nothing, so the Holy Trinity shall make all well that is not well" (ST: 15, 24). Everything that is is like a "little thing, the size of a hazel-nut"; the universe forever and before seems to Julian "so small" it "might suddenly disappear" (3, 7). The cross of Jesus Christ is the source of human one-ing in such a way that it is both nonnecessary and definitive. I will try to put that simply: The cross did not *have to be*. God made everything from nothing, and so creation did not *have to be*. The cross is also the definition of everything that is, so that you and I and Tom Joad and anyone suffering under any system that renders us nothing know ourselves saved. We are saved not by our suffering. My suffering is not necessary. Jesus Christ allows me to feel and know and see that my suffering has not rendered my life meaningless. I have not been eternally dismembered by pain or eternally forgotten by the accidents of the absurdist world around me.

Jesus's suffering means that he knows all of his kin. He knows those who have had their shame exposed and those who have been executed as public examples of shame and those who bear a shame that isolates them from God, from their loved ones, and from themselves. Jesus pulls all of us into a fissure in time that may shape our bodies for joy, safety, and courage. Recall that Julian has seen "a great union between Christ and us" (ST: 10, 17). This union has pulled all of our pain and suffering toward the cross.

Here, in this part of Julian's reflections on her visions, she says that Jesus is joyful that what he endured is endured forever and ever. The cross, as God's work of salvation in time, is both complete and infinitely expansive. Jesus says (in my words), *Dear God, let this isolating and terrifying suffering never be expected of anyone or glorified in anyone or glorified as necessary by anyone ever again. It is finished, and it has shaped everything before and since.* Jesus says (again, in my paraphrase and interpretation), *What I did stands for all time as never to be repeated.*

Turner wrote his pithy article and book focused carefully on what Julian means when she writes that sin is "behovely." The Middle English word is a contentious word to translate; according to one translation, Julian has seen that sin is "necessary." A better word, Turner (2004, 416–20) writes, is "fitting." In Turner's reading, Julian's use of "behovely" in relation to sin is embedded in the affirmation of "a God" who "so devises a 'plot' whose sole meaning is 'love'" (420). He suggests that in the way Julian situates human sin, sin becomes "behovely" or "fitting" as part of a story. I would emphasize along with Turner that the "fitting" Julian sees has the cross as the center around which all other parts of the story revolve. The cross is gratuitous, non-necessary, and a creation of love out of the non-sense and nonnecessity of evil. When I recognize and experience my body as revolving around that completely unnecessary—but now fitting—profligate gift of love, I release my anxiety and shame about having been beset by the evil around me.

The phrase I have used for this final chapter of the book is "nakedly and truly." This phrase comes early for Julian, in the Short Text, chapter 17. Here she is thinking through how God has shown to her that he receives our confession in such a way that our shame is healed: "Although a man has the scars of healed wounds, when he appears before God they do not deface but ennoble him" (ST: 17, 26). It is not as if the process of confession is magic. I still bear the scars of the wounds that someone else has caused and the wounds that I have caused my-self. But I can come before God with my fully unabashed humanity, trusting that Jesus has known the worst that I have known and that I am never alone in what I have endured or in what I have inflicted. I am not sure exactly what this means; I am still trying to learn. I think it means something like standing in front of a mirror, naked, and see-ing myself as though so absolutely safe and totally beloved that I am *unappraised*. The standards of evaluation are taken away, and I receive a vision of myself as God sees me: immeasurably glorified.

Knowing that God is not viewing us with scorn but is ready to heal us and be kin with us, we may show ourselves "nakedly and truly" to God. Julian envisions the world held safe in such a way that "sin is not shameful to man, but his glory" (ST: 17, 26). In this passage she touches upon one of the most radical implications of her text: the glory of those whose lives are obviously marked by the fall and suffer-ing of humanity. Naming David, Peter and Paul, Thomas the twin, and Mary Magdalene, Julian concludes that "it is no shame to them that they have sinned . . . for there the badge of their sin is changed into glory" (17, 26). Fear of the suffering brought on by the fall and fear of the fall itself are transformed, as Christ pulls all near. Drawing on this passage Bauerschmidt (1999, 123) writes that, in Julian's vision, "the structure of the social body of Christ gives pride of place not to those who possess the most power, but to those who have been most in need and received the greatest mercy."

In my own experience, and in my experience hearing from other people who have survived something that threatens to make their lives meaningless—without any way to make meaning—one aspect of suffering is a feeling of being singled out and alone. Although I have known people to ask, "Why, God?" in the wake of suffering or in the middle of it, there is a response that is sheer and utter humiliation. People can sometimes be so shaped by the vortex of meaninglessness that a *why* is impossible. To risk *why* sends me back into a past of mis-takes and, often, shame. Julian's vision of sin "changed into glory" is a redirection away from any question of *why* or a desperate evasion of *why* into a different space.

Later, in the Long Text, from the epigraph to this chapter, Julian asks her readers to "think hard" about what it means that Jesus has told her, in a vision, that it is his "delight" that he has "ever endured suffering for you" (LT: 22, 72). She writes, "What I am describing causes Jesus such great pleasure that he thinks nothing of all his hardship and his bitter suffering and his cruel and shameful death" (22, 73). This takes us back to the way Julian sees the cross as safety, but also as joy. I believe Julian shows the cross as safety and as God's joy in a way that is singular. The cross is repetitively given to us in the Lord's Supper, but Jesus's sacrifice is that one *poynte* through which all of us are pulled for our safety and joy. This may mean that Jesus's suffering invites his followers powerfully to refuse a cautious, calculated distance from suffering. Julian's emphasis on "ever" here, and her insistence that we stay right there on that word, is key. In her description time is brought together so that the cross is layered also with joy. The suffering of Jesus Christ in the Passion is brought together with the "numerous joys" that are the end of suffering, our being "brought" up to "heaven," and our being "bought" away from the "endless torments of hell."

At the beginning of her story Julian does not ask for the wounds of Jesus Christ in order to experience suffering as a thing in and of itself. She asks for the wounds of Jesus Christ in order to receive a full sense of the joy that has been brought into the world through Jesus. That Jesus suffered is a given. The cross is the bloody truth of sin. The cross is also the bloody truth of God's abundant, floor-soaking love, poured out. The sign of the cross, or the significance, is layered, brought into one *poynte*, so that those who concentrate on the cross may experience reassurance and even delight.

This may mean that those who follow Jesus are brave in the face of potential persecution, suffering, disease, and shame. Such holy foolhardiness in the face of evil does not mean Christians are to go seeking out situations of horror or pain. But neither do we run in the other direction or distract ourselves from the misery or domination of people around us. This holy foolhardiness may reflect the true estimation that, when we are being treated like mere things or like tools or like toys in the hands of a sadistic child, the cross may be a focal point for our courage to resist. The cross may bring us the grace to refuse the implicit or explicit ways we measure ourselves and read ourselves as measured, whether that worldly and mistaken mode of measuring leads us to be falsely exalted or ignored or humiliated. The incalculable gift of grace refuses metrics and may bring to us the courage to see the details of structural and individual sin around us.

My older daughter wrote me something beautiful after finding out the meaning of the word *profligate*. It is a word I have used often in teaching. In a text message on her phone she wrote these words, which I have her permission to share: "Honestly, I didn't really understand the word profligate in the past, but I looked it up for a paper and I LOVE that you use it in reference to grace. What a wonderful image. So much love and grace from God that it washes over us recklessly. We don't have to conserve or save grace from God because WE are already saved with abundant and unending grace."

My daughter loves math, and she loves solving puzzles. She inherited this from my mother, whose idea of fun is reading complicated spy novels by one of those British authors whose plots are so byzantine I cannot begin to keep up. Julian is a systematic theologian, as Turner has thoroughly noted. Yet one of the truths that Julian is so intent to sort through analytically requires that we loosen our hold on the accustomed tools for following a labyrinthine plot or winning a competition of survival. God's recklessness, to paraphrase my daughter, may inspire a holy recklessness in our own souls. Caroline Walker Bynum (2007, 207) writes about the sacred scrambling of economics and stations in Julian's visions, "Blood is to Julian neither substitute for debt owed nor sacrifice offered up. It is enkindling, but it is more than proffered example or arousal. Flowing blood is the locus of life and joy. As Julian says explicitly, love is the answer. Blood is love." To combine Bynum with my daughter's text, Jesus's blood is not part of an economic calculation at all. It is recklessly given and constantly flowing.

Recall again that during Julian's time people who were not part of the clergy did not receive the blood from the cup in the Eucharist. They received only the bread, the body of Jesus, and only on special occasions and in an elaborate spectacle that reinforced the order of the aristocratic hierarchy. She writes, "He has brought us up to heaven and made us his crown." If God is all love, and the Fiend has been conquered, and we are all held in God's palm, then, by one provocative and powerful reading of Julian's visions, we are all kinned, knit together as part of God's crown. Julian does not say that God brings us up to heaven to remind us, for all time, that God is God and we are decidedly not God-like. Julian does not follow a line pursued by some popular writers today that shores up God's power by reinforcing our humility and underscoring division and submission. Julian says that we, we mere laity or mere women or just mere sinners, are God's crown and God's "endless delight." God endlessly delights in us, you and me—and us—kinned in a manner that challenges how God's people, in England, in Julian's time, received the body of Jesus Christ.

If you and I are together part of God's crown, then God's spectacle of profligate abundance often appears backward, or at least mixed up. The Lord's Supper is a mixed-up blessing of kinning, so that we see one another as siblings and as each, incalculably, part of God's beautiful, exquisitely unique crown. It then would become nonsensical for a Christian to tell anyone, in any church, that she is most accurately estimated as part of God's feet or hands or toenails. If we are all part of the crown of God, that means we may see truthfully how we treat one another like feet or toenails after we leave the Lord's Supper.

In his 1995 essay on vernacular theology Watson says that, toward the end of Julian's life, one of the arguments circulating against translating Scripture and theological texts into English was that it would allow people of the "lower order" to depend less fully on "Christians of higher order." Using a compilation of documents on translation issues (edited by Margaret Deanesly), Watson points out that one opponent of allowing regular people to read and argue about theology insisted it would be like allowing a "foot or a hand" to read. That is, it would be nonsensical because neither feet nor hands have eyes. "The clergy represent the eyes of the mystical body of Christ," and nonclergy are incapable of seeing, by this logic (841). One way to understand the importance of Julian's vernacular theology is to say that she was a foot who made clear that she had eyes. She had visions, and her visions match the form of her writing. She is part of Mother Church, which makes her part of the body of Christ, and she was part of what we might call the social body in a way that marked her as common. Her visions of the body of Christ marked her in a totally different way than she was supposed to be marked. Julian was mundane, and she was given eyes to see and words to speak.

During his first year of teaching at Duke a friend of mine protested the silliness of dividing people up by "lower" and "higher." We were being told exactly the order of arrival for walking into a grand spectacle of academic excellence. I am not categorically against long, flowing robes and fancy hats. But the ways the hierarchy of a university intertwines with Christian language would make a member of the Order of the Masons blush. To quote Williams (2000, 6) again on the shape of bodies in grace, "The only secure reality is something almost absurdly different, the anarchic mercy of God, which ignores order, rank and merit." This beloved colleague arrived his first year bemused by the whole southern Christian–plus–Gothic aesthetic going on. In a faculty meeting he asked, point blank, whether Jesus would approve of the way we were entering a place of ostensible Christian worship. In other words, he asked whether Jesus would recognize our entry into the chapel as worship. Or would Jesus see our liturgy as a fancy reinforcement of the rungs on the ladder of a hierarchy? He suggested that Jesus would probably tell us to walk into chapel as we arrive or as we want to, or at least not as part of a strict ranking of who is who and who should be walking and talking with whom or singing the opening hymn alongside whom.

You would have thought he had suggested an orgy. He did not mean to cause a ruckus, but he started one. After much wrangling, we voted to go into any formal ceremony at Duke Chapel according to awkward attention to Jesus. You might walk in next to an administrative assistant who makes your copies but whose name you cannot remember. You might walk into chapel at the tail end of the line because we were all waiting for you and you did not show up in time to be toward the front. (But we still love you.) By Julian's logic, we are all part of the crown of God. I think this colleague would want me to attribute his courage to the extraordinary whimsy of the Holy Spirit. This may seem like a small story about the silliness that is the academy, but it is a snippet of how our bodies may be marked as gracefully different from the markings of station assigned to us. It took courage for this colleague to point out how silly our assembly of bodies had become.

One reasonable reaction to a colossal spectacle of suffering such as the Great Plague, the consistent domination of the English feudal system, famine, 9/11, or the war on terror and terrorism itself is fear. As I have taught Julian for fifteen years, the news has been everywhere in the United States drenched in the sweat of fear. Julian received an entrance into visions of the crucifixion and received a courage that is strange. She did not receive the sort of courage that made her titanium. Blood, not impermeable armor, is love. One response to suffering would be to build up a layer of protection from any potential intruder, seeing each person as a possible danger. What happens to our bodies in the crucifixion is a safety that may give us a way to trust and not run away from truth, whether that running away is distraction from the world or steeling ourselves from the pain of the world and the suffering of others around us. Our task is not to try to be stronger than or impervious to the evil around us. Julian's version of safety is not Wonder Woman with a lasso or a warrior princess with a herd of dragons. Her version of safety makes us part of God's crown, and that crown is on a savior who is also like a nurse, caring for children.

When I was a young teenager in West Texas, the most popular books for girls my age were by Judy Blume. My two daughters are now fourteen and twenty. The books and movies marketed to them are apocalyptic survival stories. One series is written by a woman who grew up Mormon and who apparently thinks that sexual attraction involves killing. Another series is written by a woman who thinks the future requires a young woman to know how best to shoot other young people through the heart with a longbow. Yet another series tells a girl or young woman to learn how to sacrifice herself, because, after all, that is the highest form of love. The books and movies aimed at girls and young women that receive the most press right now involve the worst sort of analytics about who will die, who will survive, and how to judge with whom to mate. That is not the freedom the gospel tells me is ours.

The visions Julian received require us to think not only about how we see the world around us but what we seek to put in front of our eyeballs. In this last chapter I am going to risk jumping off of Julian's text, using her visions as a way to interpret the unreality of what passes as political realism for many of my youngest students and often for my daughters' peers. Williams (2000, 6) writes that, in St. Paul's distinction between perceiving God as admonishment and perceiving God as good news, "self-dependence is revealed as a mechanism of self-destruction; to cling to it in the face of God's invitation to trust is a thinly-veiled self-hatred." One way to interpret the popularity of television shows and movies that depict in grueling detail forms of violent domination, especially after 9/11, is to view this viewing as self-hatred and lack of trust. It seems some viewers have wanted to focus on suffering in a way that is like a self-cutting or self-exposure to controllable displays of desolation.

Two television series that feature bodies in time in a way different from Julian's repetitive, profligate grace are 24 and *Game of Thrones*. 24 is a torture-procedural, starring one central hero who repeatedly saves the country by dominating and systematically dismembering other people. *Game of Thrones* is a pseudo-medieval fantasy with monsters and gory royal maneuverings. *Game of Thrones*, like 24, plays on themes of temporality and fear of the future ticking forward into apocalypse. 24 begins each episode with a map of the United States and a clock ticking. The opening sequence of *Game of Thrones* features an intricate, moving, miniature map of the fantasy land and a medievalesque globe-dial, resembling an astrolabe, spinning toward the resumption of another brutal, indefinitely enduring winter. The clock is ticking. In both series it is a time of urgency and suffering, when men and women must act to save the future. Because *Game of Thrones* is also part of a resurgence of medievalphilia in the United States, it seems particularly helpful to consider its popularity during a time when public beheadings and burnings and plague on other continents are part of the daily news cycle in the mainstream U.S. media. The first season of *Game of Thrones* sets up a worldview wherein kinship and friendship connections are simultaneously crucial and violently relinquished in the preparations for an apocalyptic winter. In the midst of impending hell on earth, viewers are drawn in to see the unique vulnerabilities and gifts of cursory characters and compelled to watch while these individuals are graphically killed.

The liturgical refrain of *Game of Thrones* is "Winter is coming." The Christian, liturgical calendar celebrates the anticipated arrival of Jesus, born of Mary, in a stable, at Christmas. And, again, Jesus, beloved of Mary, resurrected in a way that confuses all of the men around him, at Easter. I recently, inadvertently, gave the Benediction at a worship service in a way that directly countered *Game of Thrones*. I had watched one season of the show in order to fulfill a commitment I had given in 2010 to write an essay on torture and television in the United States, and the refrain apparently stuck like bubblegum music on my brain. Realizing only that morning that I was expected to give the Benediction after I had delivered a difficult sermon, I said, "Be courageous. Easter is coming."

I had inadvertently but directly countered the message of the series. Winter is always coming. Spring will come again.

The apocalyptic has been used again and again and again to frighten people to be obedient or pragmatic or despondent. Julian has helped me to proclaim (and, much more important, to believe) that Easter is more real than any impending apocalypse.

Game of Thrones is fantasy, and, although any military analyst will tell you 24 is fantastical, 24 is not strictly within the fantasy genre. But Game of Thrones is like 24 in its emphasis on a crisis of impending doom and in the way its violence is intertwined with sex, power, masculinity, and femininity. Many of the admirers of Game of Thrones suggest that the repeated scenes wherein women are sexually violated are warranted because they are "realistic" to the vaguely designated time period in which the fairy tale is set, that is, once upon a time, in a medievalesque land far, far away. As with another popular television show of the new millennium set in an earlier era, Mad Men, the abysmal treatment of women seems to provide masochistic/sadistic viewing pleasure justified somehow by purported historical accuracy. The messages similarly undergird a gender binary of strength vulnerability, encouraging emotional distance and preparing viewers to suffer loss, steel themselves against suffering, and yet still end up beheaded or impaled. Asceticism in the face of austerity is also basic to Game of Thrones. It is not incidental that the unequivocal, unambiguous heroes of the first season are soldiers sworn to monastic celibacy. And, following scene after repetitive scene of naked female love-slaves, the heroine of the first season must suffocate her rapist-husband-turned-lover. She then emerges naked but unscathed from a fire, a fire in which another, older woman is ritually burned to death (while screaming for mercy, no less).

This is bloody untruth. Reading Julian might help diagnose this turn toward violence. The form of self-hatred that Williams writes about in this sentence is not gender-specific: "Self-dependence is revealed as a mechanism of self-destruction; to cling to it in the face of God's invitation to trust is a thinly-veiled self-hatred." But I want to turn to specific connections between fear of social anarchy, the blessing that Julian receives, and fear of femininity and female sexuality. How is lack of trust in Jesus manifest in the kinds of self-hatred and self-destruction going on in a state of perpetual war, repeatedly broadcast threats of terror, and apocalyptic warnings about the coming famine and winter of climate change? What does it do to us when our primal stories are about danger, sacrifice, bondage, and competition? Diagnosing these connections has been important for my own life and teaching, both as a woman and as a survivor of physical and psychological abuse. I have found that both men and women, younger and older, have found these connections helpful. The pressure to be Superman or to find Superman, or the pressure to be a dragon princess or raise your daughter to be one—these seem to throw many people into anxieties that are hard to shake off. Julian's visions provide a redirection of vision. She invites us to recognize our symptoms of hypervigilance and its twin temptation: medicated denial.

Recall that Julian completed her Long Text at an intersection that Watson describes as a clamp-down. Watson (1995, 831) writes that the moves to proscribe vernacular theology at the beginning of the fifteenth century led to "silent compliance" and "self-censorship" for the sake of public order or "the common good" and for the sake of a writer's own safety. The governmental and church authorities, when they were not warring against one another, colluded to prompt fear and reinforce the current order.

The book that has helped me to think about the mobilization of fear as a way to control people today is by Corey Robin (2004). In *Fear: The History of a Political Idea* he writes that fear is an instrument of control, and he describes two different ways that governing leaders produce and manipulate fear.[1] Robin explains that one way people in power can use fear as a tool of control is by designating "public objects of apprehension and concern." In this way "the nation or some other presumably cohesive community" is encouraged to define itself as people who rec-

1. Leaders also use fear to manipulate and control one another. That message will be in my next book.

ognize the danger of "a foreign enemy or some other approximation of the alien, like drugs, criminals, or immigrants." The second way that political leaders may use fear depends on and reinforces "the social, political, and economic hierarchies that divide a people." The "specific purpose" of this second sort of fear is "intimidation, to use sanctions or the threat of sanctions to ensure that one group retains or augments its power at the expense of another." He continues, "Where the first mode of fear involves a collective's fear of faraway dangers or of objects, like a foreign enemy, separate from the collective, this second mode of political fear is more intimate and less fabulist, arising from the vertical conflicts and cleavages endemic to a society. . . . This second kind of political fear grows out of and helps perpetuate these inequities, which are so helpful to their beneficiaries and so detrimental to their victims." In this way, fear "qualifies as a basic mode of social and political control" (18). When he uses the word *mode*, Robin is talking about a combination of intentional method and intentional direction.

Robin reminds his readers that fear is not only something that naturally happens as they go about their daily lives. Fear is also something that can be used to make people compliant or resentful, despondent, cruel, or isolated. What Robin means when he says that this second mode (or method) of fear is less "fabulist" is that it is more subtle. This form of fear is not wearing a bad haircut or a giant Dixie flag. The mode of fear that manipulates our relationship to one another inside a neighborhood or a family or a city is often subtle, a form of self-censorship, and, to borrow Watson's words, uses "silent compliance." The first mode of fear—fear of an outsider or outsiders—is obvious. Think of the various ways people are taught to worry about aliens on the big screen at the movie theater, whether those aliens speak Arabic or Spanish or come in on a spaceship. When televisions were blaring "Ebola" and "ISIS" all over the United States before the midterm elections in 2014, this was a form of the first, fabulist use of fear, replete with mythic images of blood, foreign people climbing over walls, and lots of gore. The ways that internal forms of fear work are more subtle than external specters of fear, and these internal forms are more subtle today than they were during Julian's time.

When King Henry IV approved a statute in 1401 called *De heretico comburendo*, ordering that anyone holding heretical views or books with heretical views would be burned, its aim was not opaque or hidden. The document clearly stated that the aim of the statute was to "strike fear" across the country. People were supposed to be afraid. Today this form of manipulation through fear uses the assumptions of "common sense" about race or economic distress or what makes a real woman a real woman or a real man a real man. This form of manipulation reinforces these structures by reminding people what they are "really" supposed to believe about themselves and one another if they are going to pass for normal.

In Julian's time Norwich was a central port city, where fears about strangers arriving from elsewhere could be usefully intertwined with fears about one's own neighbor, servant, lover, or child. Today those whose clothing marks them as Muslim or whose accent marks them as Latino or Latina can tell stories about how people have reacted to them as alien while they are just walking down the street to the grocery store. The two modes of fear, of outsiders and of troublemakers in our midst, are intertwined in the lives of many people in the United States. We are like one big, swirling port city. Robin helps me to think about how our own versions of sumptuary laws function today. Recall that sumptuary laws defined what clothing each class was supposed to wear. These rules can become so much a part of our everyday mental life that we are divided from one another and taught to be in competition with one another without recognizing it at the front, most aware part of our souls. This is the "divide and conquer" mode of political manipulation. Julian's time was soaked in this way of manipulating people's fears and in overt, obvious ways.

Julian's vision of kinned bodies may help to wake us up to the more subtle modes of manipulating our fears and nightmares. Her visions may help us name the fears that have encouraged us to accept torture as necessary or to think of sex as fundamentally anarchic or to look at people who struggle financially as drains on the economy or to think of children born into poverty as accidental or to view immigrant families who speak Spanish as possible carriers of disease and cultural contamination. You can come up with your own list. These are a few that have come to me as I teach Julian to students in North Carolina.

I want to focus on one more level of particularity, on how this form of fear-as-manipulation functions in relation to women, and to my body in my particularity as a woman. What does it mean that fear of being vulnerable, or feminine, may be manipulated to encourage fear and division between men and women, between women and women, and between men and men? Again, I have found such helpful insight into the possible implications of Julian's writing by reading another non-Christian writer. The political theorist Michelle Goldberg (2009) writes in her book *The Means of Reproduction* about the way that fear of sexual anarchy within a group of people can be manipulated so that women try to police other women and control themselves for the sake of holding onto some semblance of safety and order. Goldberg and Robin each look unflinchingly at the way fear and domination function in the United States after 9/11. Here is Goldberg, writing in the conclusion of her book:

> The history of our species is, by and large, a history of male domination. The subordination of women, and their reduction to their reproductive function, has been such a constant that it can appear somehow normal and right, while the upending of old roles seems to cause a disorientating chaos. All over the planet people are reacting to the confusing, bumptious world wrought by globalization by clinging ever more tightly to tradition, or to the illusion of tradition. Emancipated women become a symbol of everything maddening and unmooring about modernity. To tame them seems a first step to taming an unruly world. (244)

Julian's visions of kinship are consonant with a solidarity that refuses fear of human authority. She may elicit our recognition that fears of political reprisal may be a demonic form of controlling people. Reading Julian in this way helps me question whether fear of reprisal is a proper motivation for holy self-regulation. I need to regulate myself in certain ways particular to my personality, but that should be a matter primarily before God, not because I walk around afraid that someone is going to scold, shame, arrest, or hit me. If Jesus Christ is our safety, and that safety comes through the cross, then clinging to safety by focusing on certain bodies as uniquely treacherous or chaotic, and therefore as objects for regulation, is a sign of self-loathing and mistrust in God. Jesus Christ is my safety. That safety comes through the cross. If my body has become caught in the crosshairs of worldly authority, then something has gone wrong.

Reading Julian together with Goldberg has helped me to name a trend I have seen within some Christian circles. I am not claiming that Julian herself would see this aspect of Christian sexuality, but that reading Julian has helped me to name this as a problem facing Christians. This strand of argumentation within some Christian circles identifies sex as chaotic and pregnancy as punishment. In this askew way of thinking, sexuality is anarchic, or at least dangerously aimless, unless sexual desire is aimed in particular and explicitly toward pregnancy. Pregnancy is what recalibrates and orders what would otherwise be a force for social disintegration. This deep distrust in human bodies, in our blood and our bones and our passions, can lead to a form of thinking that renders bodies primarily sites for control, to keep the archways of heaven from falling down on us. By this askew way of seeing, control of sexuality, and of women's bodies in particular, may keep the gates of hell from swallowing us all up. Or, to use Goldberg's metaphors, making children primarily a punishment for sex becomes a way to "moor" the world and to "tame" the menace of evil. Control of procreation or reproduction provides an anchor for our ship if we are feeling that we are morally at sea.

This is a gnarled-up twist of a significant strand in Christian body politics, and it distorts the witness that sexuality is a source of joy and that children are a gift, not a punishment. When this strand starts by being twisted together with fear of sexuality, children can become cast as a due punishment for desire—an act of justice that, if circumvented, supposedly can turn God's creation into a mess of wanton abandon.

I have to give credit where credit is due. My oldest daughter pointed this out years ago at a pro-life event where I had been invited to speak. She was about twelve at the time, and sorting through her own sense of sexuality. I had done a fairly good job, I pray, in conveying that her body is not dangerously ridden with desire but beautifully created by a God who wants her to know joy. In conversation with the men at the occasion (and men significantly outnumbered women at this particular event), she picked up on the sense that, for too many of them, pregnancy is retribution for sexuality itself. She picked up on the fact that too many of the men there had a loathing toward sexuality and a sense that sexuality without due consequence is the root of many other evils. She used the term *creepy* to summarize the feeling of the setting. She was right. It *was* creepy.

This creepy way of thinking may be particularly attractive during times of generalized fear over matters that have nothing to do with whether or not a woman wants to have non-procreative sex with her beloved. When people cannot find work, when elders have a sense that things are changing too fast, when more and more of my neighbors speak a different language than mine, when we fight two brutal wars that seem to have resolved nothing, well, maybe at least we can make women who have sex pay their due. I am not saying this is a conscious, front-of-the-brain sort of impulse. It is often buried deep down in the moral gut of a Christian imagination. Restore societal order by making this one core fact of life "simple" again: Sex = Baby.

In the visceral logic of this thinking, cutting social programs for women and children may, for some pro-life people, make perfect sense. Why should others be forced to pay for your individual inability to control your sexual desire, or for your community's inability properly to discipline your people's desire? Children are the consequence of your urges, and you should pay for their food, education, and care yourself. Or your community, neighborhood, or culture has become wanton with sexual anarchy, and the right way to correct this is for you people to have to bear more babies and begin to deal with the due consequences of your sexual anarchy. At the time of my writing, mainstream news sites are reviving a form of this argument that certain communities, particularly African American neighborhoods, are culturally chaotic and require instruction and discipline. A form of argumentation about a "culture of poverty" among African Americans comes right back up in the United States whenever there is a resurgence of resistance to racialized oppression. This is the pro-life version of the "your child, your choice, your responsibility" economics that I named, in a book called *Conceiving Parenthood*, as a danger also within liberalism.

This is to mistake the control of women's bodies and women's sexuality as the source of security against chaos and as safety from evil. The site of safety is not my vagina. The site of safety is Jesus. The site of safety is the unrepeatable yet perpetually repeated gift of Jesus on the cross. The liturgy of salvation is the Lord's Supper, where we receive this gift and know ourselves placed at the intersection of God's joy and God's "anarchic mercy," to repeat Williams.

It is helpful to read Williams (2002) again, this time from his lecture "The Body's Grace," given at the end of the 1980s, to consider how true sexual intimacy involves vulnerable openness and courage to perceive our bodies as freed and sustained not through outside intervention to discipline and punish but through patient attention to one another. Such patient attention is not the business of outside disciplinarians or authorities.

> The discovery of sexual joy and of a pattern of living in which that joy is accessible must involve the insecurities of "exposed spontaneity." . . . I can only fully discover the body's grace in taking time, the time needed for a mutual recognition that my partner and I are not simply passive instruments to each other. Such things are learned in the fabric of a whole relation of converse and cooperation; yet of course the more time taken the longer a kind of risk endures. There is more to expose, and a *sustaining* of the will to let oneself be formed by the perceptions of another. Properly understood, sexual faithfulness is not an avoidance of risk, but the

creation of a context in which grace can abound because there is a commitment not to run away from the perception of another. (315)

A friend who had escaped an abusive marriage told me that it took her a long time not to feel haunted by the presence of the abuser when she was with her new lover. A message of tightened-up control is obviously off the mark for men and women who have survived abuse from someone who was supposed to be their beloved. For those who have experienced something that threatens to make their body feel cursed, dirty, fallen, or forgotten, allowing another person to see them naked is a miracle. The "commitment not to run away from the perception of another" involves courage to risk also being perceived. What Williams is describing requires similar courage for men and women who have been brought up to perceive themselves as viewed by someone ready to scold or arrest them for masturbating or holding hands or simply dressing in a way that might be perceived as gender-bending or as sexually charged. When your story is such that you bring a fear of domination into a space of sexual intimacy, the challenge may be to trust that God is blocking the front door of your apartment, holding back the army of shame, and silently cheering you on toward joy. This may be precisely how someone may perceive God, in Jesus Christ, holding all that is, safely, as a mother whose sole attention is on our being made well.

Margaret Atwood has written several novels that explore the intersection of women's bodies, fear of social chaos, and domination. She writes speculative fiction in order to highlight dynamics that are part of the everydayness that many people in North America take to be normal. *The Handmaid's Tale* was published in 1985: "It was after the catastrophe, when they shot the president and machine-gunned the Congress and the army declared a state of emergency. They blamed it on the Islamic fanatics. . . . Keep calm. . . . Everything is under control. . . . There wasn't even any rioting" (1998, 174). The narrator is a woman readers only know by the name given to her by the new regime: Offred. That is, "of Fred," meaning Fred's concubine. As the narrator,

Offred has a voice, even though she has no apparent say in her enslavement. At the close of the book she has risked the possibility of actual, not forced, intimacy with another man and also the possibility of real friendship with another concubine. Fearing a public spectacle of torture, she is brought to a point of utter desperation. The world she lives in almost necessitates that such trust will lead to public humiliation and death. She writes, "Dear God, I think, I will do anything you like. Now that you've let me off, I'll obliterate myself, if that's what you really want; I'll empty myself, truly, become a chalice. . . . I'll accept my lot. I'll sacrifice. I'll repent. I'll abdicate. I'll renounce. . . . Everything they taught at the Red Center, everything I've resisted, comes flooding in. . . . I want to keep on living, in any form" (286).

It is at this point that the stakes of falsified faith become stark to readers who have learned Scripture in their own vernacular. Offred has been trained to hear a truncated version of Scripture. Along with all other women in this dystopia, Offred is forbidden to read words on a page. The Bible she hears is in the form of snippets, read out loud by someone assigned to teach control, with a perpetual refrain of meekness and submission. In Atwood's book, services of union come straight from the most misogynist parts of a letter in the New Testament called First Timothy. In the world of The Handmaid's Tale, anything we would usually think of as desire for true sexual intimacy is channeled toward the control of the stratified and strictly regulated population.

Reading Julian alongside Atwood underscores the importance of Julian's visions of divine love—both the particularities of those visions and the vernacular form of them. It matters that women read and that we not read truncated, directed forms of a complicated tradition. Atwood's world of fear is predicated on the notion that women's sexuality is to be controlled and that control of sexuality is a crucial mode for reinforcing a hierarchical order. Reading Atwood's speculative fiction alongside Julian's visions has taught me to hope in the recurrence of courage under domination, and, in Atwood's MaddAddam trilogy, she brings Julian herself directly to bear on what it means to think inside a *poynte* that recalibrates space and time. The heroine of the second and third books describes a despondency different from Offred's but one that also may resonate with contemporary readers: "We're using up the Earth. It's almost gone. You can't live with such fears and keep on whistling. The waiting builds up in you like a tide. You start wanting it to be done with. You find yourself saying to the sky, Just do it. Do your worst. Get it over with. She could feel the coming tremor of it running through her spine, asleep or awake" (2010, 239).

The first book of the trilogy, *Oryx and Crake*, ends by asking whether human beings are more worth saving than killing. *The Year of the Flood*, the second of the three books, ends with an annual feast of Saint Julian and All Souls, drawing on Julian of Norwich, and there Atwood repeats the question. She avers in all of these books that there is no evidence we are more or less prone to incinerate ourselves in a climate apocalypse or a war for mere survival. But the liturgy for Saint Julian and All Souls includes these words: "As always on this day, the words of Saint Julian of Norwich, that compassionate fourteenth-century Saint, remind us of the fragility of our cosmos—a fragility affirmed anew by the physicists of the twentieth century, when Science discovered the vast spaces of emptiness that lie, not only within the atoms, but between the stars. What is our Cosmos but a snowflake? What is it but a piece of lace?" (2010, 423–24).

She then quotes Julian's vision of the hazelnut "lying in the palm of my hand. . . . It lasts and ever shall, for God loves it." Atwood ends the second book with Julian, and the toss-up of trust or fear results in the survival of two characters anyone with any practical sense would want dead. She brings Julian of Norwich back in to thread the final book, *MaddAddam*, in a nonsensical miracle involving liturgical, chimerical pigs. (Yes, pigs.)

To find that a world so intertwined with horror is also potentially a miracle, I must release my hold on what I usually think of as truth. I must see the world askew. As Atwood asks, "What is our Cosmos but a snowflake? What is it but a piece of lace?" There is no mercantilist estimation that can count holy sanguinity as true. To see the fragility of our lives as akin to lace requires, at least for me, a continual readjustment of vision and a continued affirmation of courage.

Perhaps the most controversial part of Williams's "The Body's Grace" is the fact that he actually uses the word *clitoris* in an essay on grace. Methodists sing during Advent a carol with a line that goes "Lo, he abhors not the virgin's womb." Growing up singing about Jesus not abhorring a virgin's womb is the closest I remember getting to talk about women's bodies in church. And I will be honest, I do not know if I would have the courage to type the word *clitoris* into a book if a white man in an ecclesially authoritative hat had not typed it first. That is how deeply I am immersed in the patriarchal mess of Christendom. But Williams did type it, and he suggests in the lecture (now essay) that the fact that God created women with a nonnecessary part of our bodies, meant for pleasure, suggests that sexuality is not always and everywhere a matter of our bodily use-value for keeping order or keeping the generations generating: "It puts the question which is also raised for some kinds of moralists by the existence of the clitoris in women; something whose function is joy. If the creator were quite so instrumentalist in 'his' attitude to sexuality, these hints of prodigality and redundancy in the way the whole thing works might cause us to worry about whether he was, after all, in full rational control of it. But if God made us for joy . . . ?" (2002, 318–19).

That Jesus is our safety, and we are knit together as God's crown, and that the Lord's Supper mixes up bloodlines in such a way that the church practices holy miscegenation—all of these affirmations from Julian's visions come to bear on the collective body of my beloved Durham, North Carolina, and my individual body sitting here in my living room. Our lives, marked for safety and for courage, are not "meant" for any project. My existence, and all that is, are both unnecessary and fitting. I could have not been, but I am. And this fitting-ness is held safely in God's palm. What Williams calls "hints of prod-igality and redundancy," I have found repeatedly in Julian's visions of God's love. The *Revelations* she received centuries ago may recalibrate our visions so that we refuse to have our bodies put at cross-purposes against one another. She receives a form of love that demobilizes shame and may, with practice, allow for glimpses of holy solidarity.

The back-and-forth of receiving grace and receiving the courage of solidarity with other real people is still confusing to me. Many days I wake up with just enough energy to give love and kindness to the im-mediate people I must encounter. I wake up some days having to pray for the energy to be gracious to my own daughters and their need of me. Usually, not always, those hardest days are the ones when I am really unclear about God's omniamity for me. So I keep turning back to trying to trust in God's love. A stanza from a favorite hymn of mine goes like this:

Jesus, Bread of life, I pray thee,
let me gladly here obey thee;
never to my hurt invited,
be thy love with love requited;
from this banquet let me measure,
Lord, how vast and deep its treasure;
through the gifts thou here dost give me,
as thy guest in heaven receive me. (Franck, 1989)

The miracle that is the banquet of the Bread of life, this body of Christ strewn all over the planet on tables of Communion each time people receive the Lord's Supper—that miracle is my best experience that my love for God is not unrequited. This requires of me that I invite God precisely to my hurt, and to find me immeasurably loveable. The twentieth-century poet Delmore Schwartz (1989) has a section from his volume *Last and Lost Poems* that I learned to read in this way, as a love song from God. While typing this, the words feel awkward. How could God be so omni-amorous as to sing me a love song?

I Aria

"—Kiss me there where pride is glittering
Kiss me where I am ripened and round fruit
Kiss me wherever, however, I am supple, bare and flare
(Let the bell be rung as long as I am young:
let ring and fly like a great bronze wing!)

"—I'll kiss you wherever you think you are poor,
Wherever you shudder, feeling striped or barred,
Because you think you are bloodless, skinny or marred:
Until, until
your gaze has been stilled—
Until you are shamed again no more!
I'll kiss you until your body and soul
the mind in the body being fulfilled—
Suspend their dread and civil war!"

Toward the end of her Long Text, Julian delineates four kinds of fear before God. She assumes that the only possible good form of fear is fear in the face of God, but then she specifies that fear before God is useful only if it is properly "reverent." And here is how she defines properly "reverent": she explains that other forms of fear before God may "appear to be holy" but be "not truly so" if fear tempts us to hide our bodies from God. "The fear which makes us quickly flee from all that is not good and fall upon our Lord's breast like a child upon its mother's bosom"—that is the form of fear that is holy. This "fear" is the result of "knowing God's everlasting goodness and his blessed love" (LT: 74, 163). As she wrote much earlier, at the end of her Short Text, "For reverent fear, the more we have it, the more it softens and comforts and pleases and rests us; and the false fear disquiets, distresses and disturbs" (ST: 25, 38). Amy Appleford (2008, 194) explains in her treatment of Julian's relation to medieval practices of devotion that Julian changes a language of fear into a language of love: "Christ, no longer a necessary defender of the abject sinner, offers to Moriens [that is, to every mortal person], not protection from divine anger, but the shelter of a lover's arms." By my reading, Julian has transformed the word *fear* into a sense of intimacy with God's ability to see and forgive and love the ways that our bodies and minds have been locked into a "dread and civil war." This is the fear of God that sends me running, unabashed, toward God.

POSTSCRIPT

Growing up in West Texas as a Methodist preacher's daughter, I had lived in seven different towns by sixth grade. With each move, my mother would need to economize, to spare the next church any extra expense. A story my mom often told me concerned pioneer women who had to choose just one beautiful, superfluous item to pack into the wagon going west. A china teacup, a treasured book of poetry, a necklace handed down from an aunt—this was the sort of little, non-necessary thing a woman might find room for as she tried to pack the wagon as lightly as possible.

French-braiding my hair, my mom would intertwine stories of pioneer women with the 1940s popular song "Buttons and Bows," a cowgirl version of the cowboy classic "Bury Me Not on the Lone Prairie." The lyrics to "Buttons and Bows" go like this:

> East is east and west is west
> And the wrong one I have chose;
> Let's go where I'll keep on wearin'
> Those frills and flowers and buttons and bows,
> Rings and things and buttons and bows.
> Don't bury me in this prairie.
> Take me where the cement grows;
> Let's move down to some big town

Where they love a gal by the cut o' her clothes,
And I'll stand out in buttons and bows.
(Livingston and Evans, 1947)

The song was written by two men from Pennsylvania and became a hit by way of a movie with Roy Rogers, Jane Russell, and Bob Hope, *The Paleface*, during World War II and immediately afterward. It was their version of the medieval painting of the gathering-up of dismembered people at the end of time. A somewhat academic-sounding phrase for this that I think is pretty enough to use is "eschatological reclamation." My mother was singing a song of eschatological reclamation. *Eschatology* means, literally, words about the end, or words about the end of time. *Reclamation* is a helpful word to put alongside *eschatology* because it announces that we are going to be reclaimed, claimed and brought together by God.

"Bury Me Not on the Lone Prairie" is also known as "A Cowboy's Lament." In the original song, circulated in the first few decades of the twentieth century, a young man asks not to be buried alone, so far from home, where the "coyotes howl and the wind blows free." The specter of being buried in a shallow grave, exposed by the wind, and then eaten by coyotes, is in the cowboy song's lyrics. "Buttons and Bows" may have resonated with women who were rationing everything at home, wondering whether their sweetheart, husband, or son was going to come home—and, whether, when, or if they did come home, they would be like the previous generation of survivors. Would they return psychically dismembered like so many of the veterans who survived the horrors of World War I? Like other zany musicals of the World War II era, the song may have served as both a sparkling distraction and an acknowledgment of the fragility of life.

Let my life be meaningful, the song suggests. Traveling wherever necessary in order to be married to an itinerant preacher, my mom knew what it was like to gather up buttons and bows. She saved up those bits and pieces of beauty to sew into handmade dresses for me. I know that sounds like a country music song, but it is true.

This question of eschatological reclamation has puzzled many

Western philosophers. May someone plausibly desire heaven? Will all the beautiful buttons and bows and best thoughts and desiccated cowboys and cowgirls of this life be brought together to have infinite, coherent meaning? Some people need Christian faith to be analytically reasonable in order to keep it. The answer to this question—whether all we see as truly good will not be ultimately lost—depends on a different way of counting time than is analytically defensible.

Both of my daughters have asked me questions about time and reclamation. My older daughter told me that it was hard not to see her existence as part of a mistake once her father and I divorced. My younger daughter asked me, one Ash Wednesday, whether I regret marrying her father. These conversations each happened while I was driving down the highway, and I listened and responded as best I could. In the first case I just listened. My older daughter is biologically "mine," in that she is the result of sex that her father and I had. She may have been asking me, implicitly, how I now evaluate that time in my life. And, honestly, I still do not have an answer for her. I know unqualifiedly that I love her. My younger daughter is adopted, and so her questions are differently complicated. She asked me whether, if I had a time machine and I could turn back time, I would *not* marry her father. I have asked myself the same question on and off now for two decades. I told her that I am grateful that time does not work that way. I am grateful that I cannot turn back time. I am grateful that I am not the grandmaster of my own time. She and her sister are the most amazing blessings in my life, and I cannot imagine life without them.

This is part of the truth that Turner answers in his query about providence and evil. Julian says that "sin is behovely," or "fitting," and Turner (2004, 2011) spends much time explaining in careful, analytic detail what this means. Part of what Julian means, according to Turner, is that sin is a given, a truly horrible reality that you cannot go around or give an accounting for. But sin does not mean that life is so absurd that our existence is stripped of daily meaning. The plague, abuse, domination, and the abomination that is the intertwining of faith and violence in Julian's turn-of-the-century England—these do not mean that life is so absurd that catapulting my thinking backward into impossible "what if's" makes sense. The fitting of sin into the repetitive, cyclical, trustworthy story of God's salvation allows me to put one foot in front of the other and discover daily beauty in the world. Sin does not break open the fissures of the universe and make life itself so confusing as to not be worth living. Sin has not made the world so thoroughly incomprehensible as to be not worth risking the love of people who are also flawed and mortal.

A paraphrase of Julian that a friend shared with me, though not in any official translation, is truthful in a Julianesque sense:

The worst has happened, and has been repaired.

This obstinate hope requires a consistent affirmation that bears are going to barf up arms and coyotes are going to vomit up lost cowboys. Marilynne Robinson is best known for her Pulitzer Prize–winning novel, *Gilead*. Her first novel, *Housekeeping*, is a story deep with detailed loss. One section of the novel is the inspiration for my term *eschatological reclamation*: "There would be a general reclaiming of fallen buttons and misplaced spectacles, of neighbors and kin, till time and error and accident were undone, and the world became comprehensible and whole. . . . What are all these fragments for, if not to be knit up finally?" (1980, 92).

What are all these fragments that are our limbs and livers and loves if not to be knit up finally? Julian's visions are not finished. Her visions hint toward a universal and particular eschatological reclamation—a reclamation of the little things and a reclamation of everyone. She has not herself been given a full vision of exhaustive completion, and she says as much: "This book was begun by God's gift and his grace, but it seems to me that it is not yet completed" (LT: 86, 179). The "not yet completed" is an invitation to read and to keep thinking along with her. I also add this word, which comes before Julian declares the end of her visions:

He did not say, "You shall not be tormented, you shall not be troubled, you shall not be grieved," but he said, "You shall not be overcome." (LT: 68, 155)

A Summary of Julian's Visions

If you are the sort of person who prefers graph paper to collage, it may be helpful to have a detailed list of Julian's visions. I have written this book with her visions layered on top of one another, like a kaleidoscope. Especially in her Long Text, Julian does not write like a cartographer plotting a map or, to use a different metaphor, as a ladder upward to heaven. But for more analytically inclined readers, a list may help you summon the patience to learn how to see through her kaleidoscope. I am indebted to the editors of the Penguin edition for the idea of providing the visions as a list.

While in her bed sick, Julian stares at the cross that her pastor has put in front of her. She asks God for "a bodily sight" and sees "suddenly" blood flowing from Jesus's crown of thorns. She writes later of this vision, "[I] saw in my mind . . . that I, yes, and every creature living that would be saved, could have strength to resist all the fiends of hell and all spiritual enemies" (ST: 3, 6–7).

Julian says that "at the same time" she saw this, she saw "a spiritual vision of his familiar love" and also "a little thing, the size of a hazel-nut, lying in the palm of my hand" (ST: 4, 7). She sees that this little thing is everything, and that it exists because God loves it.

God shows Julian "our Lady," or "Lady Saint Mary," and Julian repeats that the hazelnut is "so small I thought it might have disappeared" (ST: 4, 8).

Still looking "on the crucifix which hung before me," Julian sees Jesus in "many lingering pains" and, in this, sees that "everything which is done is well done" and that "sin is nothing" (ST: 8, 12).

Julian watches as again Jesus is "bleeding abundantly, hot and freshly and vividly" and, in contemplating what she has seen, is shown that "with his Passion he defeats the Devil." It is here that she laughs at the Devil (ST: 8, 13).

She sees Jesus suffering, and specifically suffering in a sort of desiccation, being bled dry on the cross. In the midst of this she sees "a great union between Christ and us; for when he was in pain, we were in pain" (ST: 10, 16–17).

Julian sees three heavens and "complete joy in Christ," followed by a sense of "delight" that "the Holy Trinity feels in our salvation" (ST: 12, 18–19). Jesus shows her blood flowing from his side. God asks if she would like to see "Lady Saint Mary," and she does see her, three times (13, 20). Soon after, she receives the words "But all shall be well, and all manner of things shall be well" and understands this to be God filling her with "compassion for all my fellow Christians" (13, 22). God repeats the affirmation of "wellness" in the next several chapters (15–16) and affirms to her, "I am keeping you very safe" (17, 25).

After seeing and smelling the Devil tormenting her, God "opened my spiritual eyes and showed me my soul in the middle of my heart." Julian sees her soul "as large as if it were a kingdom" and that Jesus has made her soul "his most familiar home and his favourite dwelling" (ST: 22, 33).

Julian sees the Holy Trinity in such a way that "love is nearest to us all" (ST: 24, 37). She then sees four different forms of fear, one of which allows us to be "secure in love" (25: 37–38).

Somehow, in the mix of years praying about and sorting through the sense of what she has seen, Julian has a new sense of clarity about a vision of a fallen Servant and a pleased Lord. She describes this vision and the implications of her vision only in her Long Text, chapters 52–58.

REFERENCES

Aers, David. 2009. *Salvation and Sin: Augustine, Langland, and Fourteenth-Century Theology.* South Bend, IN: University of Notre Dame Press.

Aers, David, and Lynn Staley. 1996. *The Powers of the Holy: Religion, Politics, and Gender in Late Medieval English Culture.* University Park: Pennsylvania State University Press.

The Ancrene Riwle. 1990. Translated by M. B. Salu. Exeter, UK: University of Exeter Press.

Appleford, Amy. 2008. "'The Comene Course of Prayers': Julian of Norwich and Late Medieval Death Culture." *Journal of English and Germanic Philology* 107.2: 190–214.

Atwood, Margaret. 1998. *The Handmaid's Tale.* New York: Anchor Books.

Atwood, Margaret. 2003. *Oryx and Crake.* New York: Anchor Books.

Atwood, Margaret. 2010. *The Year of the Flood.* New York: Anchor Books.

Atwood, Margaret. 2014. *MaddAddam.* New York: Anchor Books.

Bauerschmidt, Frederick Christian. 1999. *Julian of Norwich and the Mystical Body Politic of Christ.* South Bend, IN: University of Notre Dame Press.

Bynum, Caroline Walker. 2007. *Wonderful Blood: Theology and Practice in Late Medieval Northern Germany and Beyond.* Philadelphia: University of Pennsylvania Press.

Coontz, Stephanie. 2000. *The Way We Never Were: American Families and the Nostalgia Trap.* New York: Basic Books.

Faludi, Susan. 2008. *The Terror Dream: Fear and Fantasy in Post–9/11 America.* London: Atlantic.

Franck, Johann. 1989. "Deck Thyself, My Soul, with Gladness." 1649. Translated by Catherine Winkworth, 1863. In *The United Methodist Hymnal*. Nashville: United Methodist Publishing House.

Given-Wilson, Chris, Paul Brand, Seymour Phillips, Mark Ormrod, Geoffrey Martin, Anne Curry, and Rosemary Horrox, eds. 2005. *Parliament Rolls of Medieval England*. British History Online. Accessed December 22, 2017. http://www.british-history.ac.uk/no-series/parliament-rolls-medieval.

Goldberg, Michelle. 2009. *The Means of Reproduction: Sex, Power, and the Future of the World*. New York: Penguin.

Guthrie, Woody. 1940. "Tom Joad—Part 2." *Dust Bowl Ballads*. RCA Victor.

Jantzen, Grace M. 1988. *Julian of Norwich: Mystic and Theologian*. Mahwah, NJ: Paulist Press.

Julian of Norwich. 1998. *Revelations of Divine Love*. Translated by Elizabeth Spearing. Introduction and notes by A. C. Spearing. London: Penguin Books.

Klein, Naomi. 2007. *The Shock Doctrine: The Rise of Disaster Capitalism*. New York: Metropolitan Books.

Levertov, Denise. 1997. *The Stream and the Sapphire: Selected Poems on Religious Themes*. New York: New Directions.

Livingston, Jay, and Ray Evans. 1947. "Buttons and Bows." Columbia Records.

Miller, Vassar. 1991. *If I Had Wheels or Love: Collected Poems of Vassar Miller*. Dallas: Southern Methodist University Press.

O'Donnell, James. 2006. *Augustine, Sinner and Saint: A New Biography*. New York: Harper Perennial.

Piper, John. 2009. "The Young and the Reformed." Panel discussion. Religious Newswriters Association Conference, Minneapolis, September 11.

Robin, Corey. 2004. *Fear: The History of a Political Idea*. New York: Oxford University Press.

Robinson, Marilynne. 1980. *Housekeeping*. New York: Picador.

Robinson, Marilynne. 2004. *Gilead*. New York: Farrar, Straus and Giroux.

Schwartz, Delmore. 1989. *Last and Lost Poems*. Edited by Robert Phillips. New York: New Directions.

Turner, Denys. 2004. "'Sin Is Behovely' in Julian of Norwich's *Revelations of Divine Love*." *Modern Theology* 20.3: 407–22.

Turner, Denys. 2011. *Julian of Norwich, Theologian*. New Haven: Yale University Press.

Valente, Catherynne M. 2008. "Rules for Anchorites." July 11. *Catvalente*. http://catvalente.livejournal.com/371419.html.

Watson, Nicholas. 1991. *Richard Rolle and the Invention of Authority*. Cambridge, UK: Cambridge University Press.

Watson, Nicholas. 1995. "Censorship and Cultural Change in Late-Medieval England: Vernacular Theology, the Oxford Translation Debate, and Arundel's Constitutions of 1409." *Speculum* 70.4: 822–64.

Watson, Nicholas, and Jacqueline Jenkins, eds. 2006. *The Writings of Julian of Norwich: A Vision Showed to a Devout Woman and A Revelation of Love*. University Park: Pennsylvania State University Press.

Williams, Rowan. 2000. *The Wound of Knowledge: A Theological History from the New Testament to Luther and St. John of the Cross*. Eugene, OR: Wipf and Stock.

Williams, Rowan. 2002. "The Body's Grace." In *Theology and Sexuality: Classic and Contemporary Readings*, edited by Eugene Rogers, 309–21. New York: Wiley-Blackwell.

INDEX